Prophet Uncovered Completely

Prophet Joshua Holmes

JHM

ISBN: 1979215855
ISBN-13: 978-1979215855

JHM©
Joshua Holmes Ministry
Facebook: Prophet Joshua Holmes
Twitter: @JoshuaHolmes777
Instagram: @ProphetJoshuaHolmes
Periscope: @Joshuaholmes777

CHAPTERS

112 WISDOM QUOTES OF PROPHET JOSHUA HOLMES

1. "IF GOD DOESN'T CHANGE THE TROUBLE YOU ARE IN...
IT IS BECAUSE HE IS CHANGING YOU IN THE TROUBLE."

2. "YOU WILL NEVER HAVE JOY...
FOCUSING ON SOMEONE WHO HAS BEEN SENT TO STEAL IT FROM YOU."

3. "DELAYED OBEDIENCE... DELAYS SEASONS.

4. "WISDOM AVOIDS... WHAT BIRTHS A STRUGGLE."

5. "THE ANOINTING... IN YOU IS FOR YOU.
THE ANOINTING... ON YOU IS FOR OTHERS."

6. "DON'T LET PEOPLE CHANGE YOU FROM LOVING GOD...BECAUSE LOVING GOD CHANGES PEOPLE."

7. "WHATEVER YOU RECEIVE IN YOUR SPIRIT, YOU WILL RECEIVE IN YOUR FUTURE."

8. "IF YOU DON'T WANT IT TO MANIFEST IN YOUR FUTURE... DON'T LET IT MANIFEST IN YOUR THOUGHTS."

9. "THE DANGER OF NOT LETTING GOD GROW YOU... IS EVEN WHAT YOU HAVE GROWN WILL BE LOST."

10. "DISTRACTION CREATES SUBTRACTION."

11. "IF A WRONG DECISION NEVER DIES... YOU WILL DIE INSTEAD."

12. "EVERY BAD THOUGHT SHOULD HAVE A FUNERAL."

13. "YOUR THOUGHTS DECIDE WHICH KINGDOM PROCEEDS OUT OF YOU. GOD'S KINGDOM OR SATANS KINGDOM."

14. "IF YOUR ANOINTING IS NOT MAINTAINED... IT WILL PRODUCE PAIN."

15. "GRACE DOESN'T REPLACE OBEDIENCE."

16. "REPENTANCE DELIVERS YOU FROM A DEMON... CONTINUAL REPENTANCE KILLS A DEMON."

17. "STRUGGLE CREATES CONFUSION... AND CONFUSION ALWAYS KEEPS YOU IN STRUGGLE."

18. "IF YOU MOVE FASTER THAN GOD... YOU BECOME SLOW TO DEMONS."

19. "ELISHA DID NOT GO BEFORE ELIJAH... HE WENT BEHIND ELIJAH."

20. "ANXIETY GOES BEFORE A MAN OF GOD. HUMILITY GOES BEHIND A MAN OF GOD."

21. "PRIDE PROVIDES... DEADLY HARVESTS."

22. "GOD REPLACES A WRONG PERSON... BY FINDING A STRONG PERSON."

23. "A TRUE PROPHET MAKES YOU SHIFT. A FALSE PROPHET MAKES YOU DRIFT."

24. "IF YOU GET STRESSED AROUND A MAN OF GOD... YOUR REBELLION IS CAUSING IT."

25. "NEVER LET YOUR EYES... PRODUCE A COVENANT WITH LIES."

26. "A WOMAN WITH VIRTUE... WILL NEVER HURT YOU."

27. "LAUGHTER INVITES GOD... TO STOP YOUR DISASTER."

28. "WHATVER KILLS THE FEAR OF GOD... KILLS THE FAVOR OF GOD."

29. "WHATEVER DOESN'T GROW YOU... SLOWS YOU."

30. "DON'T INCREASE IN DOING... ANYTHING THAT DOESN'T INCREASE YOU."

31. "REMEMBER WHAT INSPIRES YOUR SURRENDER."

32. "SOME ATTACK GOD... SOME ATTRACT

GOD."

33. "GRATITUDE IS… THE CONQUERER OF WRONG REACTIONS."

34. "THE END OF A WRONG RELATIONSHIP… IS THE BEGINNING OF A SUPERNATURAL RELATIONSHIP."

35. "WHATEVER CREATES PAIN… IS TEMPORARY WHEN YOU RECEIVE GOD'S WISDOM."

36. "WISDOM CREATES A PATH… FOR YOU TO LAUGH."

37. "DON'T LOOK AT WHAT INTRODUCES DEPRESSION."

38. "DEPRESSION STOPS PRESSING TOWARDS THE FINISH LINE."

39. "STRESS IS OVERTHINKING… WHAT GOD DOESN'T WANT YOU TO THINK OVER."

40. "STRONG FOCUS PRODUCES STRONG ANOINTING."

41. "THE DEMONS AT THE END OF A

DIVINE ASSIGNMENT... WILL BE GREATER THAN THE DEMONS AT THE BEGINNING OF A DIVINE ASSIGNMENT."

42. "LONELINESS IS... THE REACH FOR SOMEONE THAT GOD REMOVED.

43. "ANXIETY MAKES GOD'S TIMING AN ENEMY."

44. "WEAKNESS IS... THE REMEMBRANCE OF WHAT SATAN SAID."

45. "IF YOU QUIT STOPPING... YOU WILL STOP QUITTING.

46. "NO CAN DEFEAT YOU... WHEN YOU STAY IN YOUR ANOINTING."

47. "THE PERSON GOD SENDS TO YOUR LIFE... WILL NOT PUT AN END TO YOUR LIFE.

48. "ENJOY YOUR ASSIGNMENT AND GOD WILL GIVE YOU MORE ASSIGNMENTS YOU ENJOY."

49. "SOME ARE ASSIGNED TO KEEP YOU FOCUSED...
SOME ARE ASSIGNED TO MAKE YOU LOSE

IT."

50. "PROPHESYING THE WORD OF GOD TO YOURSELF... INCREASES JOY."

51. "YOUR ENEMY INSPIRES GOD TO PREPARE YOUR TABLE."

52. "THOSE THAT TALK FOR YOU... WILL ALWAYS BE HATED BY THOSE WHO TALK AGAINST YOU."

53. "PRAISE REMOVES DEPRESSION."

54. "PURSUING GOD... IS THE KEY TO SUBDUING THE ENEMY."

55. "VASHTI WILL ALWAYS HATE ESTHER."

56. "THE DISTRACTED WOMAN... WILL ALWAYS ENVY THE ATTENTIVE WOMAN."

57. "LOYALTY MAKES YOU A TARGET FOR DEMONS... BUT LOYALTY WILL PROTECT YOU FROM DEMONS THAT TARGET."

58. "DON'T LOSE PASSION... WHEN GOD DOESN'T DO IT YOUR WAY."

59. "CONSISTENT ATTITUDES... PRODUCE CONSISTENT FAVOR."

60. "IF YOU CAN CONTROL YOUR MOUTH... YOU CAN CONTROL YOUR LIFE.

61. "ENTERTAINING ANGELS IS BETTER THAN ENTERTAINING DEMONS."

62. "WHATEVER LEAVES YOU... IS NOT WORTH CHASING AFTER."

63. "A NEW LIFE... REQUIRES A NEW FOCUS."

64. "DISCOURAGEMENT IS... THE ABSENCE OF REVELATION."

65. "THE BEAUTY OF A WOMAN... IS HER ABILITY TO HELP."

66. "A MAN'S DOMINION... IS RELEASED WHEN HE SERVES SOMEONE ELSE."

67. "KINGS LOVE HUMILITY."

68. "KINGS DESIRE LOYALTY."

69. "KINGS LONG FOR THOSE WHO FEAR GOD."

70. "HONOR IS TREATING SOMEONE THE

SAME WAY GOD WANTS THEM TREATED."
71. "CURIOUSITY CAN CREATE ROADS
THAT GOD NEVER WANTED YOU
TRAVEL."

72. "WHEN YOU ARE CURIOUS... IT CAN
BIRTH HAZARDOUS DECISIONS."

73. "THE PATH WHERE YOU ARE
ATTACKED... IS THE PATH YOU WILL BE
PROMOTED."

74. "REAL QUEENS... SUBMIT TO REAL
KINGS."

75. "THE ANOINTING FOR YESTERDAY...
WAS ONLY FOR YESTERDAY."

76. "THINKING DAYS AHEAD... DESTROYS
PRESENT PEACE."

77. "DIVINE WOMEN... LOVE DIVINE
THOUGHTS."

78. "BEHIND EVERY VIRTUOUS WOMAN...
THERE IS A VIRTUOUS MAN."

79. "JEALOUSY IS AN ISSUE SOMEONE
HAS... IT IS NOT YOUR JOB TO FIX."

80. LAZINESS ALWAYS HATES GREATNESS.

81. "WHEN GOD SPEAKS... YOUR FAITH REAPS... MORE FAITH."

82. "BE SILENT... WHEN YOU SENSE SATAN DOWNLOADING WORDS INTO YOU."

83. "PAIN IS GOD TEACHING YOU WHAT TO NEVER RETURN TO."

84. "THE MIRROR TO THE ANOINTING... IS STUDYING SOMEONE ANOINTED."

85. "THE MINUTE YOU STOP SERVING... YOU PERMIT DEPRESSION."

86. "SERVING IS... THE DOOR TO PERSONAL HAPPINESS."

87. "KINDNESS TOWARDS OTHERS... INCREASES GOD'S KINDNESS TOWARDS YOU."

88. "WRATH PERMITS DEMONS TO TAKE OVER YOUR VOCABULARY."

89. "FAVOR DECIDES HOW FAR YOU MAKE IT IN YOUR DIVINE ASSIGNMENT.

90. "INTERCESSION IS... A INNER SESSION

WITH GOD FOR OTHERS."

91. **"JEALOUSY CREATES WRONG OBSERVATIONS ABOUT A PERSON."**

92. **"JEALOUSY TORMENTS."**

93. **"YOUR KINDNESS MOTIVATES PEOPLE TO INVEST IN YOU."**

94. **"WRATH BLINDS YOU OF THE CONSEQUENCE OF A WRONG REACTION."**

95. **"WRONG PEOPLE HAVE TO MANIFEST, IN ORDER FOR GOD TO EXALT YOU."**

96. **"REPEAT WHAT BROUGHT YOU FAVOR. DO IT BETTER THE NEXT TIME TO INCREASE FAVOR."**

97. "SOW YOUR WAY OUT OF LACK."

98. "DIVINE CONVERSATION WITH YOUR DIVINE CONNECTION... MAKES YOU MORE DIVINE."

99. "REJECTION POSITIONS YOU TO BE FOUND BY THE RIGHT PERSON."

100. "VICTIM IS... WHERE YOU ARE UNDER SATAN. VICTORY IS... WHERE SATAN IS UNDER YOU."

101. "NEVER LET THE WORDS YOU SPEAK... MAKE YOU BECOME WEAK."

102. "WHEN GOD IS READY TO PROMOTE YOU... HE NO LONGER BABIES YOU."

103. "FRUSTRATION IS WHEN YOUR MONEY IS AT A LOWER LEVEL THAN YOUR REVELATION."

104. "YOUR SEED... CREATES THE LIFESTYLE WITH GOD YOU DESIRE."

105. "RECYCLE EVERY THOUGHT THAT

MAKES YOUR FAITH EXCITED."

106. "YOUR ABILITY TO BE KIND… WILL DETERMINE YOUR ABILITY TO BE PROMOTED."

107. "FINISHING A DIVINE ASSIGNMENT… IS MORE IMPORTANT THAN BEGINNING A DIVINE ASSIGNMENT."

108. "IF YOU DON'T ENJOY YOUR POSITION… SOMEONE ELSE WILL."

109. "THE LEVEL OF YOUR DEVOTION… DECIDES THE LEVEL OF YOUR PROMOTION."

110. "SERVING A PROPHET… MAKES YOU A CARRIER OF THE ANOINTING ON THE PROPHET."

111. "IT IS WISER TO ATTEMPT PEACE… BEFORE FINALIZING WAR."

112. "STRETCH YOUR SEED… TO STRETCH YOUR HARVEST."

I CHAPTER: ANGELIC ANOINTING

ANGELS CARRY POWER BECAUSE THEY
HAVE NO SIN IN THEM.

THEY HAVE NEVER MISSED GOD.

THEY HAVE DOMINION AND AUTHORITY.

THEY CARRY ASSIGNMENTS FOR THE SONS
AND DAUGHTERS OF GOD ON THE EARTH.

THEY ARE WORKERS AND EMPLOYEES OF
JESUS, THEREFORE **MATTHEW 26:53** JESUS
SAID THAT HE CAN CALL 12 LEGIONS OF
ANGELS. ANGELS ARE HIS ASSISTANTS, THE
MINISTERS HE HAS CHOSEN TO FLOW WITH
HIM IN THE SPIRIT REALM.

JESUS ACCOMPLISHES ASSIGNMENTS IN THE
EARTH THROUGH THE ANGELS. THIS IS A
HIDDEN MYSTERY! A LOT OF PEOPLE ARE
UNAWARE OF THE ANGELIC ANOINTING.
THIS IS THE POWER IN WHICH AN ANGEL

HAS BEEN GIVEN BY GOD TO CHANGE A SITUATION IN YOUR LIFE FOR YOU THROUGH BRINGING SUPERNATURAL DELIVERANCE. THE POWER THEY WALK IN TO WIN BATTLES FOR YOU.

THE PRIVILEGE AND AUTHORITY HAS BEEN IMPARTED TO THEM BY THE LORD, TO BRING ACCURATE ANSWERS TO YOU.

THE ANGELS ASSIGNED TO YOUR LIFE ARE CO-WORKERS WITH THE HOLY SPIRIT TO CHANGE YOUR SEASON. THE ANOINTING IS UPON AN ANGEL VERY STRONGLY TO SILENCE THE ENEMY'S VOICE AND HIS ACTIVITY IN YOUR LIFE.

"HE MAKETH HIS ANGELS SPIRITS; TO HIS MINISTERS A FLAMING FIRE." (PSALM 104:4)

THIS MEANS JESUS HAS LODGED APART OF HIMSELF AND HIS DIVINE POWER INTO EACH ANGEL. ANGELS HAVE A PURE SIDE OF GOD OPERATING IN THEM.

"PURITY ALWAYS... RELEASES POWER."

THE PURITY OF AN ANGEL ALLOWS THEM TO MOVE IN INTENSE REALMS OF GOD'S POWER.

WHEN YOU HAVE A PURE HEART, YOU WILL WALK IN A GREATER ANOINTING THAN OTHERS. ANGELS CAN TURN SITUATIONS AROUND FOR YOU IF YOU KNOW HOW TO ENGAGE THEM. THEY HAVE AUTHORITY FROM GOD TO HELP YOU ON THE EARTH.

GOD'S POWER IS STRONG ON YOU WHEN YOU AVOID DECISIONS AND THOUGHTS

THAT WILL DISPLEASE THE SPIRIT OF GOD. ANGELS ARE NOT HINDERED WHEN YOU STAY FOCUSED ON JESUS AND WHO JESUS SENT TO YOU. ANGELS ARE AWARE OF THOSE WHO SAY NO TO SIN AND TEMPTATION. THEY STUDY THOSE WHO RESIST THE DEVIL.

ANGELS ARE WATCHING TO SEE WHO CAN MASTER THEIR FLESH AND CRUSH THE HEAD OF THE SERPENT.

THEY KNOW WHEN A BELIEVER MATURES AND TAKES A STAND FOR RIGHTEOUSNESS. ANGELS TAKE ACCOUNT OF WHAT YOU SAY AND DO. THEY ALSO HONOR THOSE WHO TRULY REPENT AND TURN FROM UNGODLY WAYS. THEY PASSIONATELY ENJOY THOSE THAT TURN AWAY FROM ANY ROUTE THAT IS AGAINST THE WILL OF GOD. ANGELS

TAKE NOTE OF SACRIFICIAL SURRENDER.

"ANGELS RESPECT YOU... AT THE LEVEL YOU RESPECT JESUS."

"SERVING A MAN OF GOD WITH LOYALTY, CREATES AN ANGELS LOYALTY TO YOU."

"PROPHETS CARRY LEGIONS OF ANGELS AND SERVING A PROPHET ALLOWS THESE LEGIONS OF SUPERNATURAL ANGELS TO MOVE WITH YOU."

"WHEN ANGELS SEE YOU BOW TO JESUS... THEY BOW TO YOU."

"WHEN ANGELS SEE YOU WORK FOR JESUS... THEY BEGIN TO WORK FOR YOU."

"WHEN ANGELS SEE YOU SUBMIT TO

JESUS… THEY BEGIN TO SUBMIT TO YOU."

THE SUPERNATURAL IS BROUGHT TO EARTH BY ANGELS THROUGH YOUR FAITH. YOUR FAITH ALLOWS THEM TO COME WITH THE GLORY OF GOD. IN JOHN 5 THE ANGEL CAME DOWN AND RELEASED THE HEALING POWER OF GOD. THE ANGEL WAS CARRYING THE GLORY OF GOD FOR THE PEOPLE TO BE HEALED, AND THE ANGEL RELEASED THE GLORY INTO THE POOL. WHOEVER JUMPED INTO THE WATER FIRST WAS HEALED.

THE ANGEL WAS A GLORY CARRIER AND BROUGHT THE ATMOSPHERE OF HEAVEN TO EARTH. ANGELS BIRTH GOD'S ATMOSPHERE IN THE EARTH. THEY BIRTH GOD'S ATMOSPHERE IN YOUR LIFE. IT HAS BEEN GIVEN TO YOU THE AUTHORITY, TO WELCOME ANGELS IN YOUR LIFE DAILY. DO

IT DAILY, SO YOU CAN BE EMPOWERED.
ANGELS KNOW THE WILL OF GOD FOR
YOUR LIFE. THEY HELP YOU WITH MAKING
RIGHT DECISIONS. ANGELS ARE VERY
PROPHETIC! THEY KNOW THE MIND OF GOD
CONCERNING YOUR PRESENT AND FUTURE.
PSALM 91:12 SAYS ANGELS SHALL BEAR THEE
UP IN THEIR HANDS, UNLESS YOU DASH
YOUR FOOT AGAINST A STONE.

THEY ARE THERE TO KEEP YOU FROM
FALLING INTO TEMPTATION, WRONG
DECISIONS, WRONG RELATIONSHIPS,
WRONG DIRECTIONS, AND WRONG
THOUGHTS.

PSALM 91:11 SAYS JESUS GIVES HIS ANGELS
CHARGE OVER YOU, TO KEEP YOU IN ALL
YOUR WAYS. SO THE ANGELS ARE THERE AS
CARETAKERS, TO YOUR SPIRIT, SOUL, AND

BODY. THEY HELP DEVELOP A FLOW IN YOUR CHOICES TO GUARD YOURSELF FROM WHAT WILL KILL YOUR ANOINTING. THEY UNDERSTAND WHAT IS DEADLY TO YOUR GROWTH AND YOUR GRACE. ANGELS WORK ENDLESSLY TO PREVENT YOU FROM ENTERING DANGER. THEY KNOW WHAT GOD DISLIKES AND THEY ARE ALWAYS ON BOARD MOVING YOU AWAY FROM THESE THINGS.

ANGELS ARE WITH THE HOLY SPIRIT, IN THE TIME OF CONVICTION. THEY HAVE A DEEP REVELATION ON REBELLION, SINCE THEY SAW IT FIRSTHAND IN HEAVEN WHEN LUCIFER SINNED.

THEY HAVE THE FEAR OF GOD PERFECTED WITHIN THEM, THEREFORE THEY DO NOT SIN, WILL NOT SIN, NOR DO THEY ENJOY

SEEING YOU SIN. ANGELS WILL JOIN WITH THE HOLY SPIRIT IN CONVICTING AND TELLING YOU WHAT IS WRONG. NEVER IGNORE THE WARNING OF ANGELS. THEY GIVE YOU SIGNALS. WHEN AN ANGEL IS GIVING YOU SIGNALS AND COMMUNICATING NOT TO DO SOMETHING, YOU WILL FEEL A STRANGE DETACHMENT FROM A PERSON OR PLACE.

YOU WILL FEEL THE FEAR OF GOD ARREST YOU. YOU WILL KNOW THAT THE DIRECTION IS WRONG FOR YOUR PATH. YOU WILL KNOW A PERSON IS WRONG FOR YOUR RELATIONSHIPS.

WHENEVER YOU FEEL YOURSELF GETTING OPPRESSED, DEPRESSED OR SAD… YOU NEED TO INVITE THE HOLY SPIRIT ALONG WITH YOUR ANGELS.

AN ANGEL IS A PERSON. THEY UNDERSTAND EMOTIONS, ATMOSPHERES AND WHAT IS NEEDED TO KEEP THEM ANOINTED.

THEY GRAVITATE TO GRATITUDE. THEY ADMIRE PEOPLE WHO ARE HUNGRY FOR GOD. THEY RUN TOWARDS PEOPLE WHO REPENT AND PURSUE JESUS WITH THEIR THOUGHTS AND LIFE. THEY RESPECT PEOPLE WHO OVERCOME TRIALS, TROUBLES, AND STRUGGLES. THEY OBSERVE THOSE WHO SERVE GOD CONSISTENTLY, PATIENTLY, AND CHEERFULLY WHEN THINGS ARE NOT GOING THE WAY THEY THOUGHT IT WOULD GO. ANGELS ARE VERY MUCH AWARE OF SOLDIERS IN THE KINGDOM OF GOD WHO WILL NOT QUIT, STOP, OR BE LED ASTRAY BY ANYTHING OR ANYONE WHO IS AGAINST THE WILL OF GOD FOR THEIR LIFE.

ANGELS ANSWERED JESUS SO MUCH WHILE
HE WAS ON THE EARTH, BECAUSE HE WAS
AN OBEDIENT MAN. HE LISTENED AND
SURRENDERED TO THE HOLY SPIRIT.

WHEN YOU ARE A MAN OR WOMAN THAT
YIELDS TO THE HOLY SPIRIT INSTRUCTIONS,
THERE ARE ANGELS THAT FLOCK TO YOU.
THEY SURROUND YOU. THEY CREATE
DIVINE MOMENTS FOR YOU TO RECEIVE
SURPRISE BLESSINGS AND MIRACLES FROM
PEOPLE THAT YOU MAY NOT EVEN KNOW.

ANGELS STAND ON GUARD, WAITING TO
BLESS THE PEOPLE OF GOD. WAITING TO
FIND SOMEONE THEY CAN MINISTER
BLESSINGS, FINANCES, LOVE AND
OVERFLOW TO.

ANGELS WERE MADE SPIRITS. A SPIRIT IS A PERSON. JESUS CREATED ANGELS AS SPIRITS. AN ANGEL IS A PERSON. A SPIRIT IS ETERNAL AND LIVES FOREVER.

THEREFORE, WHEN THE ANGELS FELL WITH LUCIFER GOD DID NOT DESTROY THEM.

SOME WERE PLANTED IN THE HEAVENS. SOME WERE PLANTED ON THE EARTH. SOME WERE PLANTED IN HELL, BEING RESERVED FOR THE DAY OF GOD'S WRATH. RESERVED FOR THE DAY WHERE GOD WILL FIGHT EVERY PERSON WHO REFUSED HIS SON JESUS, WHO WAS GIVEN FOR YOU TO AVOID THE WRATH OF GOD. ANGELS ARE SPIRITS THAT HAVE THE FULLNESS OF GOD MOVING IN THEM FOR THE BENEFIT OF EVERY BELIEVER. YOU CAN ONLY SEE AN ANGEL THROUGH YOUR SPIRITUAL EYES

BECAUSE AN ANGEL IS A SPIRIT.

WHEN YOU OBEY JESUS, YOU NOT ONLY ENGAGE HIM, BUT YOU ENGAGE ANGELS.

THE FLESH DOES NOT DESIRE THE MINISTRY OF ANGELS, BUT IT DESIRES THE MINISTRY OF DEMONS.

FEELINGS WILL DESTROY SENSITIVITY TO THE SPIRIT REALM OF GOD.

IT WILL KEEP YOU IN THE DEMONIC REALM OF THE FLESH. THIS IS WHERE YOUR BODY CONTROLS YOUR CONDUCT. IF YOU CAN GUARD YOUR DECISIONS FROM FEELINGS, YOU WILL HEAR JESUS CLEARER THAN EVER BEFORE. THE PROPHETIC ANOINTING IS THE HAND, BUT YOUR FOCUS ON JESUS IS THE ARM.

THE ARM HAS TO DO ITS PART… FOR THE HAND TO FUNCTION.

IF THE ARM IS CUT OFF… THE HAND CANNOT OPERATE.

THE PROPHETIC ANOINTING IS THE HAND THAT IS WAITING FOR AN ARM.

SOMEONE WHO IS FOCUSED ON JESUS WITHOUT COMPROMISE.

ANGELIC VISITATIONS IS A REWARD FOR DISCIPLINE AND HUNGER. SOMEONE WHO HAS SELF CONTROL, AND DOMINION OVER THEIR SPIRIT MAN. NOT LED BY EMOTIONS. ANGELS ARE ATTRACTED TO MADE UP MINDS. THE MIND THAT IS STAYED ON HIM. THE ESTABLISHED HEART.

DOUBLE MINDEDNESS IS THE ATMOSPHERE OF EVIL SPIRITS AND FALLEN ANGELS.

FALLEN ANGELS THEMSELVES, WERE DOUBLE MINDED BEFORE GENESIS WHERE GOD KICKED THEM OUT OF HEAVEN THROUGH MICHAEL AND HIS ANGELS.

THE SAME WAY ANGELS CAN FEED YOU... DEMONS CAN FEED YOU.

TO BE DOUBLE MINDED IS THE FOOD OF FALLEN ANGELS. ONE MINUTE THEY WORSHIPED GOD AND THE NEXT MINUTE THEY WORSHIPED THEMSELVES. THEY WERE APART OF THE 1/3 THAT REBELLED AGAINST HIM. WHENEVER YOU ARE DOUBLEMINDED, YOU ARE RECEIVING AN IMPARTATION FROM A FALLEN ANGEL.

IT MEANS AN EVIL SPIRIT HAS BECOME YOUR PROPHET.

FALLEN ANGELS UNDERSTAND THE DECEPTION OF DOUBLE MINDEDNESS.

TO BE DOUBLEMINDED MEANS YOU WERE INTRODUCED TO THE TRUTH BUT STILL BELIEVED A LIE.

FALLEN ANGELS ARE BEHIND THIS GREAT DECEPTION.
THE PURPOSE OF EVERY FALLEN ANGEL IS TO MAKE YOU LOSE YOUR POSITION LIKE THEY LOST THEIR POSITION. FALLEN ANGELS FLY IN THE ATMOSPHERE ALL THROUGHOUT THE DAY, LOOKING TO PLANT DECEPTION IN YOUR MIND. LOOKING TO SOW SEEDS OF LIES INTO YOUR HEART. THE ASSIGNMENT OF A FALLEN ANGEL IS TO CONVINCE YOU TO REJECT JESUS AND HIS PROPHETS.

"DEMONS ARE COMFORTABLE WITH BELIEVERS THAT HAVE GROWN COMFORTABLE WITH NOT CHASING AFTER JESUS AND THE ANOINTING."

"WHEN YOU LOSE THE DESIRE FOR MORE OF GOD, IT IS EVIDENCE THAT DEMONS ARE ACTIVELY MOVING THROUGH YOUR MIND AND SOUL."

THIS IS ONE OF THE MAIN REASONS WHY THE DEVIL LOVES TO KEEP YOU IN THE FLESH, BECAUSE IT TAKES AWAY YOUR SPIRITUAL VISION.

AN ANGEL HAS SUPERNATURAL ABILITIES, AS WELL AS ASSIGNMENTS. ANGELS HAVE BEEN GIVEN COMMAND BY GOD TO ASSIST YOU AND BRING YOU INTO YOUR INHERITANCE.

GOD SENDS ANGELS INTO YOUR LIFE, EVEN ACCORDING TO YOUR FAITH. ANYTHING YOU NEED; THERE IS AN ANGEL THAT CAN HELP YOU OBTAIN IT. YOUR FAITH CAN ATTRACT NEW ANGELS TO YOUR LIFE.

"WHEN YOU ARE IN FAITH, PRAISE, FASTING OR SOWING MONEY INTO THE GOSPEL... ANGELS ARE MOVING THE MOST."

THE ABILITY OF YOUR FAITH DECIDES THE ACTIVITY OF YOUR ANGEL.

IF YOUR FAITH IS VERY STRONG, ANGELIC ACTIVITY WILL BE VERY STRONG IN YOUR LIFE.

ANGELS HAVE EMPOWERMENT TO MOVE WITHOUT HINDERANCE, WHEN YOU ARE IN FAITH. WHEN YOU BELIEVE GOD AND HIS

PROPHETS, THERE IS NO DEMON SPIRIT THAT CAN DELAY AN ANGEL FROM DOING ITS ASSIGNMENT IN YOUR LIFE.

"ANGELS WAIT TO SEE FAITH… AND ONCE YOU ARE FULLY FOCUSED ON THE POWER OF JESUS, YOUR LIFE WILL TAKE OFF."

ANGELS HAVE MORE AUTHORITY THAN DEMONS… BUT CANNOT USE IT FOR YOU UNTIL YOU SURRENDER ALL TO JESUS AND LET HIM TAKE OVER.

II CHAPTER: HOW TO BREAK WITCHCRAFT IN YOUR LIFE

WITCHCRAFT IS ONE OF THE MOST SECRETIVE, DECEPTIVE, AND DANGEROUS SPIRITS OF THEM ALL.

MANY LIVE A LIFE FULL OF FRUSTRATION, DISAPPOINTMENTS, AND DELAYS WITHOUT KNOWING THE ROOT CAUSE.

WITCHCRAFT IS THE STRATEGY OF SATAN TO KEEP YOUR LIFE FROM NEVER FINISHING YOUR DIVINE ASSIGNMENT. IT IS HIS TECHNIQUE TO STOP ALL OF GOD'S BLESSINGS FROM COMING TO YOU.

WITCHCRAFT IS A COMPOUND WORD.

CRAFT IS AN ACTIVITY THAT SOMEONE HAS SKILLS IN DOING.

A WITCH IS A PERSON WHO HAS A DEMONIC ASSIGNMENT TO CAUSE EITHER YOU TO BECOME REBELLIOUS, OR CAUSE THINGS IN YOUR LIFE TO REBEL AGAINST THE PLAN OF GOD TO BLESS YOU AND GIVE YOU GOOD SUCCESS.

WHENEVER FINANCES ARE NOT FLOWING TO YOU IT IS BECAUSE OF WITCHCRAFT. WITCHCRAFT WILL STOP YOU FROM HAVING ABUNDANCE.

WHEN THINGS ARE NOT WORKING FOR YOU, AND DOORS ARE SHUTTING IN YOUR FACE IT IS BECAUSE OF WITCHCRAFT.

WITCHCRAFT WILL MAKE GOD OPPORTUNITIES FALL THROUGH. IT WILL CANCEL WHAT GOD INTENDED FOR YOUR GOOD. IT WILL MAKE YOU VERY

UNHAPPY AND UNSUCCESSFUL.

SOMEONE OR SOMETHING IS CURSING YOU.
THERE IS AN ANOINTING IN THE PROPHET
TO BREAK WITCHCRAFT OFF YOU. MOSES
BROKE WITCHCRAFT OFF THE CHILDREN
OF ISRAEL. EVEN THOUGH THEY CHOSE TO
RETURN TO IT, HIS ANOINTING SET THEM
FREE FROM THE BONDAGE AND

WITCHCRAFT OF PHARAOH. WHENEVER
THERE IS SOMETHING IN YOUR LIFE THAT
YOU CANNOT GET FREE OF, IT IS BECAUSE
OF WITCHCRAFT.

"THE EVIDENCE OF STRONGHOLDS IS
WITCHCRAFT… AND THE EVIDENCE OF
WITCHCRAFT IS STRONGHOLDS."

THOUGHTS CAN CARRY WITCHCRAFT,

ESPECIALLY WHEN THE THOUGHT CAUSES YOU TO DOUBT GOD, DISOBEY GOD, OR PROCRASTINATE WITH WHAT GOD IS TELLING YOU TO DO.

"THE THOUGHT OF WITCHCRAFT MAKES YOU ATTACK A MAN OF GOD."

"THE THOUGHTS OF WITCHCRAFT MAKES YOU DISHONOR WHO GOD SENT TO YOU."

"WITCHCRAFT THOUGHTS MAKE YOU ANGRY AT GOD, FOR THE THINGS THAT HAS HAPPENED TO YOU."

THE WEAPON OF WITCHCRAFT STARTED IN HEAVEN BEFORE GENESIS. THE BOOK OF REVELATION CHAPTER 12 EXPLAINED THAT LUCIFER DECEIVED 1/3 OF THE HOLY ANGELS INTO REBELLING AGAINST GOD. IT

WAS THE FIRST ACT OF SIN AND
DISOBEDIENCE AGAINST GOD. THIS WAS
THE BEGINNING OF WITCHCRAFT. THIS
WITCHCRAFT PRODUCED HELL AND
ETERNAL JUDGMENT FOR THE DEVIL AND
HIS ANGELS. WITCHCRAFT SET HELL IN
MOTION.

IF IT WAS NOT FOR WITCHCRAFT THERE
WOULD HAVE NEVER BEEN A HELL, LAKE
OF FIRE, ETERNAL DAMNATION, OR EVEN
JUDGMENT.

2ND PETER 2:4 ELABORATED THAT GOD
DID NOT SPARE THE ANGELS THAT SINNED,
BUT CAST THEM DOWN INTO HELL, AND
PUT THEM IN CHAINS OF DARKNESS, TO BE
THERE UNTIL THE DAY OF JUDGMENT.

HERE IS SOMETHING YOU MUST OBSERVE.

THERE WAS WITCHCRAFT THAT THE
ANGELS OPERATED IN ALONG WITH THEIR
LEADER LUCIFER. NOTICE THE NEXT
SEASON WAS HELL AND CHAINS OF
DARKNESS.

WHEN A CHILD OF GOD SINS AGAINST GOD,
WHICH IS WITCHCRAFT, HELL BECOMES
THEIR STATE OF MIND AND CHAINS OF
DARKNESS.

WHENEVER WITCHCRAFT IS MOVING IN
YOUR LIFE, YOU WILL EXPERIENCE HELL
AND CHAINS OF DARKNESS.

ALSO, IF THE CHILD OF GOD HAS NOT
SINNED AND DONE WITCHCRAFT, IT MAY
BE SOMEONE CLOSE TO THEM THAT IS IN
SIN AND DOING THE WITCHCRAFT.
WHEREVER THERE IS WITCHCRAFT, THERE

IS HELLISH EXPERIENCES AND CHAINS OF DARKNESS. YOUR ATMOSPHERE WILL BE OPPOSED FROM HAVING PEACE, JOY, LOVE, AND THE LIFE OF GOD.

CHAINS OF DARKNESS WILL BE SEEN IN YOUR PRAYER LIFE. YOU WILL NEVER BE ABLE TO FOCUS.

HELL, AND CHAINS OF DARKNESS WILL BE VISIBLE IN YOUR FINANCES. YOU WILL HAVE DEBTS, FINANCIAL DISTRESS, OVERLOAD OF BILLS, FEAR AND WORRY ALL AROUND.

HELL, AND CHAINS OF DARKNESS WILL BE IN YOUR RELATIONSHIPS. PEOPLE WILL FIGHT YOU AND TRY TO DESTROY YOU, EVEN THOUGH YOU HAVE BEEN GOOD TO THEM. YOU WILL NEVER BE ABLE TO STUDY

THE WORD. YOU WILL NEVER BE ABLE TO
WORSHIP IN SPIRIT. YOU WILL LOSE
MOTIVATION TO PRAISE GOD. YOU WILL
GO DAYS WITHOUT SPEAKING TO GOD.
YOU WILL GO DAYS WITHOUT LISTENING
TO GOD.

YOU WILL HATE PROPHETS.
YOU WILL DESPISE ANYONE THAT GOD
USES TO BE IN AUTHORITY OVER YOU.

YOU WILL LOSE INTEREST IN THE THINGS
OF GOD. YOU WILL STOP PURSUING JESUS.

YOU WILL ALWAYS BE OCCUPIED WITH
THINGS THAT EXCITE YOUR FLESHLY
NATURE. YOU WILL ALWAYS BE ANXIOUS,
OR IMPATIENT. YOU WILL ALWAYS BE
SELFISH, NEVER THINKING ABOUT OTHERS.
YOU WILL BE UNABLE TO BE STILL IN THE

PRESENCE OF GOD.
YOUR TEMPTATIONS WILL BE OUT OF
CONTROL. YOU WILL HAVE AN APPETITE
FOR THE WORLD AND WHAT THE WORLD IS
DOING. YOU WILL HANG AROUND TOXIC
PEOPLE. YOU WILL SURROUND YOURSELF
WITH GOSSIPERS AND TROUBLEMAKERS.

YOU WILL TRY TO FIT IN WITH CARNAL
PEOPLE. YOU WILL SEEK APPROVAL AND
ACCEPTANCE FROM UNGODLY PEOPLE.
YOU WILL LET ANYONE COME INTO YOUR
ATMOSPHERE WITHOUT USING YOUR
DISCERNMENT. YOU WILL OPERATE IN
YOUR FEELINGS DAILY. YOU WILL FIGHT
GOD'S TIMING. YOU WILL AVOID ANYONE
THAT CONVICTS YOU OR TELLS YOU THAT
WHAT YOU ARE DOING IS WRONG. YOU
WILL ENTERTAIN DEPRESSION AND
DISCOURAGEMENT. YOU WILL BE

STUBBORN AND PROCRASTINATE OFTEN.
THERE ARE VARIOUS SIGNS OF
WITCHCRAFT OPERATING IN YOUR SPIRIT.
YOU WANT TO BE WISE AND FLEE FROM
THESE CHARACTERISTICS.

WITCHCRAFT IS DEMONICALLY PRODUCED.

WITCHCRAFT COMES THROUGH THE
WRONG PEOPLE IN YOUR LIFE.

WITCHCRAFT INCREASES YOUR
DISTRACTIONS SO THAT YOU NEVER FOCUS
ON GOD AND DO THE INSTRUCTIONS OF
GOD. ONE MAJOR WEAPON OF WITCHCRAFT
IS PROCRASTINATION AND STUBBORNNESS.

THIS IS WHERE YOU WILL KEEP PUTTING
THINGS OFF, THAT GOD IS TELLING YOU
TO DO. THIS IS THE REALM OF WITCHCRAFT,

WHERE YOU DELAY YOURSELF.

YOU HINDER YOUR OWN BLESSINGS,
DIVINE CONNECTIONS, AND OPEN DOORS.

FEAR IS WITCHCRAFT. BEING NERVOUS IS
WITCHCRAFT.

"WITCHCRAFT IS IN ANYTHING THAT GOD
DID NOT GIVE YOU." THAT IS VERY
POWERFUL!

IF YOU RECEIVE A NECKLACE THAT GOD
DID NOT GIVE YOU, THERE ARE
WITCHCRAFT SPIRITS IN THERE.

WHATEVER YOU HAVE BEEN GIVEN, IF IT
DID NOT COME FROM GOD, THERE IS
WITCHCRAFT IN IT.

BE VERY CAREFUL OF WHAT YOU RECEIVE

FROM PEOPLE AND ALWAYS BE PRAYERFUL.

ANY CHARACTERISTIC THAT YOU HAVE, IF IT IS NOT PRODUCING THE FRUIT OF THE HOLY SPIRIT, IT IS WITCHCRAFT.

EXAMINE YOURSELF!

IT IS VERY POSSIBLE THAT YOU ARE CAUSING STORMS IN YOUR LIFE BECAUSE OF PROCRASTINATION, FEAR, AND DISOBEDIENCE.

LUST IS A FORM OF WITCHCRAFT. THIS IS A DOOR THAT SATAN USES TO ENTER YOUR LIFE, SO THAT YOU WILL NOT BE FOCUSED TO SEEK JESUS, SO THAT YOU WILL NOT HAVE CONFIDENCE TO FUNCTION IN YOUR DOMINION, AND SO YOU WILL NOT

PROSPER FINANCIALLY.

SEXUAL SIN CAN STOP FINANCES. ONCE A
DEMON CAN ENTER YOUR LIFE THROUGH
A BEHAVIOR OR THOUGHT, THEY ALSO CAN
ACCESS OTHER PARTS OF YOUR LIFE.

THEY CAN COME THROUGH ONE ENTRY,
AND USE THAT ONE ENTRY TO ENTER
SIDES OF YOUR LIFE.

NO DEMON LOVES YOUR PROSPERITY.

THE SOLE PURPOSE OF A DEMON IS TO
STOP YOU FROM PROSPERING.

YOUR PROSPERITY SHUTS THE DEVIL DOWN
COMPLETELY. THEREFORE 3RD JOHN,
CHAPTER 1, VERSE 2 SAYS THAT GOD'S
BIGGEST WISH IS FOR YOU TO PROSPER.
PROSPERITY IS SATAN'S WORST

NIGHTMARE. HE DOES NOT WANT TO SEE YOU BE SUCCESSFUL IN GOD.

YOU CAN DEFEAT ANY DEMONIC POWER, IF YOU YIELD TO THE LEADING OF THE HOLY SPIRIT AND LET HIM PROSPER YOU. DEMONS NEVER WANT TO SEE YOU EXECUTE ANYTHING THAT JESUS INSTRUCTS. THEY ARE AUTHORS OF INCONSISTENCY.

WHENEVER YOU FIND YOURSELF BEING INCONSISTENT… IT IS BECAUSE DEMONIC POWERS ARE TRYING TO RULE OVER YOU.

INCONSISTENCY IS WITCHCRAFT. WHERE YOU START DOING SOMETHING THAT PLEASES GOD, BUT THEN YOU STOP. WEARINESS IS WITCHCRAFT. THEREFORE, GOD TOLD YOU NOT TO BE WEARY IN

WELL DOING. GALATIANS 6:9

LET US NOT BE WEARY IN WELL DOING TO
AVOID BEING IN WITCHCRAFT... STAY
INSPIRED. HERE IS A SECRET... REPLAY
MOMENTS WHEN YOU FELT THE
ANOINTING.

WHETHER IT WAS FROM A SONG, A SERMON,
A PROPHECY, A PROPHET, A SERVICE, A
PERSONAL ENCOUNTER WITH JESUS, A
WORSHIP SESSION, PRAYER TIME, WHEN
YOU SOWED A SEED, WHEN YOU PRAYED IN
THE SPIRIT, PRAISED GOD, OR GOT A
REVELATION WHILE READING THE WORD
OF GOD.

"RECAPTURE MOMENTS WHERE YOU FELT
GOD STRONGLY."

"DON'T LEAVE A MOMENT WHERE THE POWER OF GOD WAS INTENSE. STAY IN THAT MOMENT MENTALLY."

"REVISIT MOMENTS WHERE YOU EXPERIENCED THE MANIFEST PRESENCE OF JESUS."

MOMENTS WHERE YOU LAUGHED. REPLAY MOMENTS WHERE YOU FELT EMPOWERED AND LOVED.

BRING YOUR MEMORY INTO TIMES OF GLADNESS, VICTORY, AND THE GOODNESS OF GOD.

THE PROPHET WILL BREAK WITCHCRAFT OFF YOU. THE GLORY ON A PROPHET CUTS OFF THE SPIRIT OF REBELLION. A PROPHET'S INSTRUCTIONS WILL SET YOU

FREE FROM WITCHCRAFT SPIRITS.
WHEN YOU STAY UNDER THE COVERING
OF YOUR PROPHET, YOU ARE PROTECTED
FROM WITCHCRAFT.

"THE VICTIMS OF WITCHCRAFT...ARE
THOSE WHO DON'T HAVE A PROPHET."

"THE ABSENCE OF A PROPHET...IS THE
ABSENCE OF A COVERING."

YOUR DECISION TO OBEY A
PROPHET...WILL DECIDE WHAT EVIL
CANNOT TOUCH YOU.

A PROPHET...IS PROTECTION.

A PROPHET...IS A PLACE OF SAFETY.

STAYING UNDER A PROPHET...IS THE

SECRET TO DEFEATING DEMONS.

III CHAPTER: GIVING YOUR SEED AN ASSIGNMENT

NEVER SOW A SEED WITHOUT HAVING
EXPECTATION FOR A HARVEST.

JESUS CREATED THE SEED PRINCIPLE FOR
YOU TO RECEIVE WHATEVER YOUR HEART
DESIRED.

YOUR SEED HAS POWER TO CONNECT YOU
TO ANYTHING THAT GOD HAS PLANNED
TO GIVE YOU IN THIS LIFE.

THE HOLY SPIRIT HAS WISDOM OF WHERE
YOUR WEALTH IS. HE KNOWS WHERE YOUR
MARRIAGE IS. HE KNOWS HOW TO RESTORE
YOUR HEALTH. HE KNOWS WHAT MAKES
YOU HAPPY AND FULFILLED. BE RECEPTIVE
OF THE VOICE OF THE HOLY SPIRIT. HE
GIVES YOU SEED INSTRUCTIONS THAT
BRING MASSIVE PRODUCTION.
YOU WILL PRODUCE INSTEAD OF REDUCE.

THE MIND OF THE HOLY SPIRIT IS ALWAYS THINKING OF "INCREASE." GOD TOLD ADAM IN GENESIS TO BE FRUITFUL AND MULTIPLY. APART OF GOD'S MINISTRY FOR ADAM WAS TO INCREASE. INCREASE IS THE VISION OF GOD FOR YOUR LIFE.

WHENEVER YOU DO NOT HAVE MUCH… YOU CANNOT DO MUCH.

LACK LIMITS YOUR ABILITY. THIS WILL BRING DELAYS TO YOUR ASSIGNMENT.

"LACK... ATTRACTS ATTACKS."

ATTACKS FROM CREDITORS.
ATTACKS FROM THE LAW.
ATTACKS FROM THOSE YOU OWE.

LACK BRING AN OPENING FOR DEMONS TO OPPRESS YOU. IT OPENS DOORS FOR ALL TYPES OF ATTACKS.

IT ATTACKS YOUR PEACE. IT ATTACKS YOUR DESIRE TO HELP OTHERS. IT ATTACKS YOUR ASSIGNMENT IN THE EARTH. IT ATTACKS YOUR MINISTRY. IT ATTACKS YOUR PRAISE TO GOD. IT ATTACKS YOUR MARRIAGE. IT ATTACKS YOUR PRAYER LIFE.

SOME PEOPLE HAVE LOST THEIR PASSION TO PRAISE GOD, PRAY, AND OBEY THE CALL OF GOD ON THEIR LIFE. THEY HAVE BECOME DISCOURAGED AND UNINSPIRED.

THIS IS FROM LACK AND FINANCIAL ISSUES. POVERTY IS A DEMON THAT DESTROYS SO MANY PEOPLE. LACK IS A VERY DANGEROUS SPIRIT. IT SUCKS ENERGY OUT

OF YOUR FAITH. IT SUCKS LIFE OUT OF
YOUR DIVINE ASSIGNMENT AND YOUR JOY.

IT INSULTS YOUR EXPECTATION.

THE SEED WILL CANCEL ALL DEMONIC
ACTIVITY AND ATTACKS IN YOUR
FINANCES.

NO EVIL SPIRIT CAN STAND UP AGAINST
SOMEONE WHO IS OBEYING GOD WITH
THEIR FINANCES.

THEREFORE, THE SATANIC KINGDOM IS
FULLY SUBMITTED TO A SOWER.
EVERY SPIRIT OF DELAY MUST SUBMIT TO A
SOWER.
WHEN YOU SOW SEEDS BY TAKING YOUR
MONEY AND RELEASING YOUR FAITH WITH
IT TO SUPPORT THE GOSPEL AND THE

MINISTRY OF JESUS ON THE EARTH,
UNSTOPPABLE BLESSINGS AND FAVOR
BEGIN TO PURSUE YOU ON THE EARTH.

THE FAVOR THAT COMES UPON YOU WHEN
YOU HONOR GOD WITH YOUR MONEY IS
ALMOST UNREAL.

THE THINGS THAT TAKE PLACE IN YOUR
LIFE SUPERNATURALLY ARE EVERYTHING
YOU HAVE DREAMED OF.

GOD BEGINS TO SPEAK TO PEOPLE ABOUT
BLESSING YOU AND DOING VERY KIND
THINGS TO OPEN DOORS FOR YOU TO
FULFILL YOUR DESTINY.

THINGS THAT HAVE BEEN SLOWED DOWN
IN YOUR LIFE, STARTS TO SPEED UP FASTER
THAN YOU KNOW. GOD WILL FLEX HIS

MUSCLES IN EVERY BATTLE THAT COMES AGAINST YOU. YOU WILL HAVE VICTORY AFTER VICTORY AND JUSTICE AFTER JUSTICE.

YOUR SORROW WILL BE TURNED TO JOY. THE SEED THAT YOU SOW NEVER DIES, IT MULTIPLIES!

GIVE YOUR SEEDS AN ASSIGNMENT.

WHENEVER YOU GIVE MONEY TO THE WORK OF GOD, THAT MONEY SEED IS A STUDENT. YOU MUST TEACH YOUR STUDENT. CHEW ON THE REVELATION THAT MONEY IS A STUDENT, THEREFORE YOU MUST TEACH IT.

"YOUR SEED... IS A STUDENT. TEACH IT WHERE TO GO, AND HOW TO RETURN TO

YOU."

WHEN YOU GIVE YOU MUST TEACH YOUR SEED WHERE IT MUST GO, AND YOU DECIDE WHERE YOU WANT THE HARVEST. YOU DECIDE WHERE YOU WANT THE INCREASE. YOU DECIDE WHERE YOU WANT THE SEED TO PENETRATE. YOU DECIDE THE SITUATION OR THE PLACE IN YOUR LIFE THAT YOU WANT THE SEED TO AIM AT TO FIX, BRING CHANGE, AND MIRACULOUS RESULTS.

TARGET YOUR SEEDS. GIVING IS ONE OF THE MOST FUN PARTS OF GOD. GOD LOVES A CHEERFUL GIVER. (2ND CORINTHIANS 9:7) WHY DOES GOD LOVES A CHEERFUL GIVER? BECAUSE IT EXCITES GOD WHEN HE SEES SOMEONE WHO IS JOYFULLY CONFIDENT IN WHAT THEIR GIVING WILL DO.

GOD LOVES TO SEE SOMEONE WHO HAS GIVEN THEIR SEED AN ASSIGNMENT. THEY ARE EXCITED ABOUT SUPPORTING THE WORK OF GOD AND THEIR HARVEST IS GREAT BECAUSE OF IT. GOD LOVES TO SEE SOMEONE WHO GIVES WITH EXPECTATION.

"YOUR DECISION TO SOW… WILL PROTECT YOU WHEN EVIL IS PRESENT."

"YOUR SEED WILL DEFEND YOU WHEN SATAN IS SEEKING TO DESTROY YOU."

"THERE ARE CHILDISH GIVERS AND CHILDLIKE GIVERS. "

CHILDISH GIVERS WILL ONLY TIP GOD. THEY WILL HAVE $10,000 AND ONLY GIVE GOD $10. THEY WILL HAVE $500 AND ONLY

GIVE GOD $5. THEY WILL HAVE 100 AND ONLY GIVE GOD $1. CHILDISH GIVERS DO NOT UNDERSTAND THE REVELATION OF THE SEED, THE SOIL, AND THE HARVEST. THEREFORE, THEY MISS BLESSINGS.

THE SEED IS WHAT YOU GIVE.
THE SOIL IS WHERE YOU ARE GIVING.
THE HARVEST IS WHAT YOU RECEIVE FROM GIVING.

TO SOW PROPER SEEDS THAT ARE LED BY THE HOLY GHOST, YOUR EYES MUST BE ENLIGHTENED AND OPENED ABOUT THE SOIL.

THE SOIL IS THE MINISTRY. IT IS THE MAN OR WOMAN OF GOD YOU ARE SOWING THE SEED INTO. THE SOIL HAS A LOT TO DO WITH WHETHER THAT SEED WILL GROW.

BAD SOIL CAN STOP YOUR SEED. WHEN YOU GIVE MONEY TO A MINISTRY THAT IS NOT GOD ORDAINED, YOUR SEED CAN BE INEFFECTIVE AND UNFRUITFUL. IF YOU SOW INTO A MINISTRY WHERE THERE ARE NO MIRACLES, NO PROPHECY, NO REVELATION, NO DEEP TEACHINGS, NO DEPTH IN THE WORD OF GOD, NO TANGIBILITY OF GOD'S PRESENCE AND POWER, YOUR SEED CAN BE QUENCHED, AND POWERLESS TO REPRODUCE.

IF A MAN HAS SEX WITH A BARREN WOMAN, EVEN THOUGH HIS SEED IS SOWN, IT WILL NOT BE FRUITFUL AND MULTIPLY A HARVEST OF A BABY. THE SEED IS HINDERED FROM PRODUCING.

THE SAME THING HAPPENS WHEN YOU SOW

WHERE GOD DID NOT ASSIGN YOU TO SOW. MAKE SURE THE MINISTRY YOU SOW INTO IS NOT BARREN. THIS IS POWERFUL!! IF YOUR SOIL DOES NOT HAVE OIL, NEITHER WILL YOUR HARVEST. THE OIL IS THE ANOINTING, AND IF THE ANOINTING IS NOT THERE ON THE MINISTRY, YOUR SEED IS BEING SOWN INTO BAD GROUND, WHICH MEANS IT WILL NOT PRODUCE. THIS IS DEADLY. ALWAYS BE IN COMMUNICATION WITH JESUS THROUGH PRAYER SO YOU ACCURATELY SOW SEED INTO GOOD SOIL.

PRAY IN THE HOLY GHOST ABOUT SOWING SEED AND THE SOIL TO SOW IT INTO. ELIJAH WAS THE SOIL FOR THE WOMAN AT ZAREPHATH. PROPHETS CARRY A HEAVY SOIL FOR MIRACLES, SIGNS, AND WONDERS. INSTANTANEOUS MIRACLES ARE IN A TRUE PROPHETS SOIL. PROPHETIC SOIL IS VERY

POWERFUL. JESUS STRONGLY MOVES IN IT.

- A TRUE PROPHET IS SOMEONE WHO PREACHES JESUS.

- A TRUE PROPHET LOVES PEOPLE.

- A TRUE PROPHET FOLLOWS THE HOLY SPIRIT.

- A TRUE PROPHET IS DEDICATED TO WINNING SOULS.

- A TRUE PROPHET IS PERSECUTED FOR THEIR OBEDIENCE TO JESUS.

- A TRUE PROPHET LIVES A HOLY LIFE EVEN WHEN THEY ARE NOT IN PUBLIC.

A TRUE PROPHET HAS BEEN THROUGH A PROCESS WITH JESUS, WHERE THEY HAVE

BEEN PERSECUTED, BETRAYED, FALSELY
ACCUSED, AND OPPOSED BY OTHERS.

"YOU DO NOT CHOOSE YOUR PROPHET;
YOUR PROPHET CHOOSES YOU."
THE WOMAN AT ZAREPHATH DID NOT
CHOOSE ELIJAH, ELIJAH CHOSE HER.

THE PROPHET WILL BE LED BY THE
SPIRIT TO MINISTER TO YOU AT THE
CENTER OF YOUR NEED.

WHEN GOD SENDS THE PROPHET TO
YOUR LIFE, THIS PROPHET WILL SUPPLY
WHAT YOU HAVE BEEN SEEKING GOD
FOR.

WHETHER IT BE JOY, HEALING,
DIRECTION, WISDOM, MARRIAGE,
DISCERNMENT, WARNING, LOVE,

FRIENDSHIP, AND FINANCIAL
INSTRUCTIONS THAT WILL BRING YOU
INTO YOUR WEALTHY PLACE.

THE PROPHET IS A GIFT FROM GOD, TO
ACCELERATE AND MANIFEST YOUR
ANSWERS TO PRAYER. THE PROPHET IS
AN ANSWER TO PRAYER.

THE SOIL OF THE PROPHET IS EMBODIED
WITH A LARGE IMPARTATION OF GOD'S
FAVOR, DELIVERANCE, AND
MANIFESTATION.

WHENEVER JESUS IS ABOUT TO BRING
YOU INTO A SUCCESSFUL PLACE, AND
PROSPER YOU IN EVERY AREA OF YOUR
LIFE, HE WILL STRATEGICALLY PLANT
THE PROPHET INTO YOUR LIFE.

THE WOMAN AT ZAREPHATH DID SOMETHING VERY POWERFUL. SHE SOWED INTO THE PROPHET'S LIFE. THIS SUPERNATURALLY CHANGED THE COURSE OF HER LIFE AND HER CHILD'S LIFE.

THE MYSTERY OF THE PROPHET'S SOIL IS REVEALED IN THIS. SHE GOES FROM HER LAST MEAL FOR HER AND HER SON, TO NEVER BEING BROKE ANOTHER DAY IN HER LIFE. THIS IS THE MIRACULOUS SOIL OF THE PROPHET.

"WHEN GOD SENDS A PROPHET TO YOU... SOW INTO HIM CONSTANTLY."

GOD CAN TAKE YOU FROM NOTHING TO SOMETHING WHEN YOU HONOR AND

HELP THE MAN OF GOD FULFILL HIS
ASSIGNMENT FROM GOD.

THERE IS A SECRET TO HOW GOD TAKES
CARE OF YOU, AND GIVES YOU MORE
THAN ENOUGH, AND IT IS THROUGH
THE SEED.

WHEN YOU SOW INTO A PROPHET, YOU
RECEIVE A PROPHET'S REWARD. THE
PROPHET'S REWARD CAME UPON THE
WOMAN AT ZAREPHATH, BECAUSE SHE
OBEYED AND GAVE HER VERY LAST TO
THE PROPHET OF GOD SENT TO HER.
WHENEVER YOU NEED A FINANCIAL
MIRACLE, GOD WILL SEND YOU A
PROPHET WITH INSTRUCTIONS.

GOD DOES NOT JUST GIVE PEOPLE
FINANCES, BUT HE GIVES YOU

INSTRUCTIONS. INSTRUCTIONS ARE CONNECTED TO THE FINANCES. IF YOU OBEY THE INSTRUCTIONS YOU WILL OBTAIN THE FINANCES, BUT IF YOU DO NOT OBEY THE INSTRUCTIONS, YOU WILL NOT OBTAIN THE FINANCES.

GOD LOVES THE WORLD… BUT PEOPLE IN THE WORLD GO THROUGH HUNGER, STARVATION, HOMELESSNESS, POVERTY, AND NEVER HAVING MONEY, BECAUSE YOU MUST OBEY GOD TO GET MONEY GOD'S WAY.

THIS WILL ACTIVATE THE BLESSINGS OF FINANCES IN YOUR LIFE.

POVERTY AND SHAME SHALL BE TO HIM THAT REFUSES INSTRUCTION (PROVERBS 13:18.)

SOWING IS YOUR WAY OUT OF POVERTY.
SOWING IS YOUR WAY OUT OF
FINANCIAL FRUSTRATION. SOWING WILL
PLACE A GRACE ON YOU TO NEVER
SUFFER HUNGER OR NEED EVER AGAIN.

IF YOU HAVE THE HOLY GHOST INSIDE
OF YOU AND YOU ARE FILLED WITH THE
HOLY GHOST, YOU WILL HATE POVERTY
AND NOT ENOUGH. THE HOLY GHOST IS
A VISIONARY, HE IS ALWAYS MOVING, HE
IS ALWAYS THINKING. IT IS APOSTOLIC
AND PROPHETIC GRACE THAT BRINGS
YOU INTO YOUR WEALTHY PLACE.
DIVINE MONEY IS REAL. BUT MATURITY,
SENSITIVITY, HONOR AND SOWING
UNLOCKS IT ON YOUR LIFE. GOD WANTS
YOU TO HAVE SO MUCH THAT
SOMETIMES YOU FEEL OVERWHELMED

WITH HIS LOVE.

"THE BLESSING... IS HOW GOD ROMANCES YOU."

THERE IS A PLACE YOUR SOUL ENTERS, WHERE DIVINE FAITH TAKES OVER. YOU BECOME EXCITED ABOUT GIVING. YOU BECOME EXCITED ABOUT SOWING SEED. YOU REJOICE IN GOD'S INSTRUCTIONS, AND HIS DIRECTIONS. HE DOES NOT HAVE TO FORCE YOU. WHEN YOU ARE IN THE FLESH DISOBEDIENCE IS AUTOMATIC. WHEN YOU ARE IN THE SPIRIT OBEDIENCE IS AUTOMATIC.

WHEN YOU ARE LED BY THE SPIRIT, YOU DO NOT NEED EVIDENCE BEFORE YOU OBEY GOD. YOU OBEY GOD BEFORE YOU HAVE EVIDENCE IN THE NATURAL.

"MOST TIMES, FAITH IS YOUR OBEDIENCE, WHEN EVIDENCE OF DELIVERANCE CANNOT BE FOUND."

"A LOT OF TIMES GOD HIDES THE SOLUTION, BUT HE HIDES IT IN THE INSTRUCTION."

THE INSTRUCTION IS SENT TO KILL YOU AND GET YOU OUT OF "YOU."
EVERY TIME YOU OBEY GOD, YOU ENGAGE HIS FINANCIAL FAVOR. THE MORE YOU SURRENDER TO JESUS, YOU ENGAGE HIS FINANCIAL POWER. PROVISION IS A REWARD FOR DYING TO YOURSELF.

JESUS CALLS YOU TO SOW YOURSELF BEFORE ANYTHING ELSE. YOU MUST GIVE YOURSELF OVER TO JESUS BEFORE YOU

CAN SOW. SOWING BRINGS YOU INTO YOUR DREAM LIFE, AND INTO THE OVERFLOW THAT JESUS HAS PROMISED YOU AS A CHILD OF THE KING.

DO NOT LET SATAN ROB YOU, OF WHAT JESUS DIED FOR YOU TO HAVE. THE DEVIL DOES EVERYTHING IN HIS POWER TO TRY TO STOP YOUR SEED, BECAUSE HE KNOWS SOWING BRINGS HIM UNDER ARREST. HE CANNOT STEAL FROM YOU ANY LONGER. PLUS, HE MUST PAY BACK EVERYTHING HE HAS BEEN STEALING FROM YOU IN YEARS PAST. THE SEED IS HIS WORST NIGHTMARE.

THE DEVIL IS SCARED FOR YOUR DOMINION TO SWITCH FROM JUST SPIRITUAL THINGS TO MATERIAL THINGS. THIS MEANS YOU ARE NOW DOMINATING IN BOTH REALMS. THE SPIRITUAL AND THE

FINANCIAL.

YOU ARE NOW IN THE BLESSING POWER OF GOD. THERE IS NOT AN AREA WHERE HE CAN DEFEAT YOU. NEITHER IN THE SPIRITUAL REALM NOR FINANCIAL REALM. THE SEED BREAKS OPEN THE HEAVENS. ONCE THE HEAVENS ARE OPENED, YOU CAN RECEIVE EVERYTHING THAT BELONGS TO YOU.

HEALTH, MARRIAGE, WEALTH, MINISTRY, AND DEBT CANCELLATION WILL COME TO YOU. YOU HAVE DOMINION THROUGH YOUR SEED TO TAKE BACK YOUR RIGHTFUL PLACE IN THIS EARTH REALM, AS WELL AS IN THE SPIRIT REALM. THE SEED ANOINTS YOU TO RECEIVE ALL THAT GOD HAS FOR YOU WITHOUT SORROW. ONCE YOU GET INTO THE FLOW OF SOWING,

NOTHING CAN STOP YOU.

GOD MAKES YOU A MAGNET FOR FAVOR, DIVINE CONNECTION, AND ABUNDANCE.

FINANCIAL STRONGHOLDS CANNOT TOUCH YOU WHEN YOU ARE SOWING, AND WHEREVER YOUR MONEY IS, IT MUST OBEY YOU AND COME TO YOU. THE EARTH AND DEMONS MUST OBEY THE SOWER AND YOUR SEED.

"YOUR OBEDIENCE WITH MONEY…IS THE SECRET TO RECEIVING MORE OF IT."

DON'T EAT YOUR SEED. SOW IT SO GOD CAN GET TO YOU MORE THAN WHAT YOU HAVE. PASS THE MONEY TEST, TO BECOME MONEY BLESSED. KEEP SOWING.

WHEN JESUS OBSERVES YOU GIVING, HE GETS COMPETITIVE AND HE STARTS OUT GIVING YOU. HE STARTS A CHALLENGE OF WHO WILL GIVE THE MOST, BUT HE KNOWS HE WILL ALWAYS WIN YOU.

AS YOU GIVE, DO IT CHEERFULLY AND BOLDLY. GOD IS TRYING TO GET SOMETHING TO YOU. DO NOT BE AFRAID TO SOW HIGHER AMOUNTS OF MONEY BECAUSE THE HIGHER YOU SOW THE HIGHER YOU REAP.

GOD DOES NOT ALLOW YOU TO BECOME POOR WHEN YOU'RE GIVING TO HIS KINGDOM. HE MAKES YOU RICH, HE MAKES YOU BLESSED, AND YOU WILL BECOME THE HEAD AND NOT THE TAIL. ABOVE AND NOT BENEATH. HE MAKES YOU THE LENDER AND NOT THE BORROWER.

THE SEED IS A SUPERNATURAL WEAPON THAT GOD HAS GIVEN YOU TO SILENCE THE ENEMY IN YOUR FINANCES AND EVERY AREA OF YOUR LIFE.

NO DEMON CAN STAND UP AGAINST YOUR SOWING ACCOUNT. NO DEMON CAN STAND UP AGAINST YOUR GIVING TO THE LORD'S WORK. YOUR SEED OFFICIALLY MUTES EVERY DEMONIC CONVERSATION GOING ON ABOUT YOUR FUTURE. YOU SHUT DOWN EVERY IDEA OF SATAN, THROUGH SOWING SEED. YOU ARE AS UNSTOPPABLE AS YOUR SEED.

"IF YOU NEVER STOP SOWING, YOU NEVER STOP GROWING, THE MONEY AND FAVOR WILL NEVER STOP FLOWING, AND THE GLORY WILL NEVER STOP SHOWING."

THE SEED TAKES YOU OUT OF THE LEAGUE OF STRUGGLING AND HUSTLING. IT GIVES YOU DEFINITE RESULTS.

WHEN YOU SOW SEED WITH ACCURACY... MEANING YOU'RE OBEYING THE HOLY SPIRIT, IT MAKES YOU REST, NOT STRESS.

DO NOT SPEND FOREVER THINKING ABOUT YOUR SEED. FOCUS ON THE HARVEST! FOCUSING ON THE HARVEST, WILL GIVE YOU GRACE TO SOW FEARLESSLY. WHEN YOU HAVE A REVELATION OF THE HARVEST, IT REMOVES FEARFUL AND SLOTHFUL RESPONSES TO SOW. MOST PEOPLE ARE AFRAID TO SOW BECAUSE THEY DO NOT KNOW THAT GOD IS GIVING THEM MORE THAN WHAT THEY HAVE. HE IS NOT

DECREASING YOU THROUGH SOWING BUT, INCREASING YOU THROUGH SOWING.

"THE SEED IS NOT TO TAKE AWAY… IT IS TO BREAK AWAY."

JESUS WANTS YOU TO BREAK AWAY FROM AVERAGE LIVING, NOT ENOUGH, BURDENS, LACK, POVERTY, AND TENSION THAT COMES WHEN YOUR MONEY IS FUNNY. YOU HAVE TOO MANY ASSIGNMENTS AND VISION FROM GOD TO STAY BROKE. YOU HAVE MAJOR TASKS THAT JESUS SHALL TRUST YOU WITH; THEREFORE, IT IS NEEDFUL FOR YOU TO HAVE WEALTH.

SOWING SEED IS LIKE A LOTTERY TICKET, WHICH IS THE WINNING NUMBER. YOU WIN EVERY TIME. NO MATTER WHAT YOUR BANK ACCOUNT SAYS.

PSALM 84:11 SAYS NO GOOD THING WILL HE WITHHOLD FROM THOSE WHO WALK UPRIGHTLY.

EVERY SEED YOU SOW COMES BACK TO YOU, GOOD MEASURE. THE MEASURE IS GOOD, NOT EVIL. MEANING GOD WILL NOT CHEAT YOU IN THE SIZE OF YOUR HARVEST.

YOU WILL ALWAYS GET BACK MORE THAN YOU GAVE, AND LIVE IN THE OVERFLOW.

GOD WILL MAKES SURE YOU GET EVERYTHING YOU SOWED FOR AND SO MUCH MORE.

YOUR HARVEST WILL BE PRESSED DOWN BECAUSE IT IS COMING FROM HEAVEN, SO

GOD MUST PRESS IT DOWN.

SHAKEN TOGETHER, BECAUSE THE LORD IS GOING TO MAKE SURE THERE IS MIXTURE OF FAVOR, GRACE, AND BLESSINGS INTO YOUR HARVEST.

RUNNING OVER… BECAUSE GOD IS GOING TO MAKE SURE YOU HAVE SO MUCH THAT YOU CAN SHOW LOVE TO SOMEONE WHO NEEDS IT. YOUR CUP SHALL RUN OVER. THE INCREASE SHALL BE SO MUCH. THE RICHES AND THE WEALTH SHALL BE SO HUGE.

YOU WILL HAVE MORE THAN WHAT YOUR EDUCATION SAID YOU CAN HAVE.
YOU WILL HAVE MORE THAN YOUR JOB SAID YOU CAN HAVE.
YOU WILL HAVE MORE THAN YOUR SALARY SAID YOU CAN HAVE.

EPHESIANS 3:20 SAYS GOD IS GOING TO DO EXCEEDINGLY, ABUNDANTLY, ABOVE ALL YOU CAN ASK OR THINK.

YOUR LACK DAYS ARE OVER!! YOUR LIMITATION DAYS ARE OVER!!

YOUR SORROW DAYS ARE OVER. YOUR DEBT DAYS ARE OVER. YOUR UNFRUITFUL DAYS ARE OVER. YOUR BROKE DAYS ARE OVER. JESUS CAME TO KILL THE STAGNATION AND FAMINE IN YOUR LIFE. HE RELEASED THE ANOINTING FOR THE GOOD LIFE, WHEN HE DIED AND ROSE AGAIN. WHEN JESUS ROSE, YOU ROSE WITH HIM. YOUR FINANCES ROSE UP. YOUR MONEY ROSE UP. YOUR HARVEST ROSE UP. YOUR INCREASE ROSE UP. YOUR PROVISION ROSE UP.

YOU WILL SEE HIS GLORY COME DOWN UPON YOU, AND YOU WILL LIVE ABOVE WHAT PEOPLE THOUGHT YOU WERE CAPABLE OF LIVING. JESUS SHALL GET THE GLORY FROM YOUR LIFE.

ALL WILL SEE THAT YOUR GOD IS GREATER, YOUR GOD IS STRONGER. HE IS A PROVIDER, THE ONE WHO MAKES RICH AND THE ONE WHO MAKES RULERS IN HIS KINGDOM. YOU ARE FLOWING IN THE SUPERNATURAL FOR FINANCES. YOU SHALL SEE GOD'S ECONOMY UPON ALL YOU DO. A NEW LEVEL OF PROSPERITY AND GOOD SUCCESS IS UPON YOU. SURELY GOODNESS AND MERCY IS FOLLOWING YOU.

THE SEED WORKS. IT IS GOD'S WEAPON. THE SEED WILL CHANGE ANYTHING IN

YOUR LIFE THAT IS CAUSING YOU DISTRESS.

THE SEED WILL BRING TURNAROUND ALL OVER.

THE SEED WILL RECOVER ALL THAT YOU HAVE LOST.

THE SEED WILL MAKE YOU RICH.

THE SEED WILL MAKE YOU OVERFLOW.

THE SEED GUARANTEES FAVOR AND FINANCES.

THE SEED IS THE SUPERNATURAL WAY TO LIVE DEBT FREE.

THE SEED WILL CONNECT YOU TO MIGHTY MEN AND WOMEN.

THE SEED IS A COVENANT THAT IS MADE…WHERE GOD PROMISES TO TAKE CARE OF YOU LAVISHLY FOR THE REST OF YOUR LIFE.

THE SEED IS A POSITION WHERE GOD CAN GET SUPERNATURAL MONEY AND PROVISION TO YOU.

THE SEED STOPS ALL SATANIC ATTACKS IN YOUR LIFE.

THE SEED CANCELS ANY CURSE THAT IS OPERATING AGAINST YOU.

THE SEED PUTS AN END TO STAGNATION.

THE SEED GIVES YOU SPEED IN THE SPIRIT.

IV CHAPTER: DEFEATING SEXUAL THOUGHTS

SEX WAS CREATED BY JESUS FOR THE PURPOSE OF FAMILY. FOR A WOMAN OF GOD AND MAN OF GOD TO ENJOY EACH OTHER. IT IS A DIVINE IDEA. IT IS A PLEASURE AND HAS A PURPOSE. THE PURPOSE IS TO REPRODUCE THE FAMILY OF GOD ON THE EARTH. FOR CHILDREN, AND FOR GOD TO HAVE OFFSPRING THAT WILL GROW UP TO SERVE HIM.
SEX IS... A REWARD SYSTEM.

SEX IS A VERY BEAUTIFUL GIFT AND IMPARTATION. IT WAS SUPPOSED TO BE A TRANSFER OF SPIRITS.

"THE SPIRIT OF GOD IN A MAN... BEING TRANSFERRED TO A WOMAN."

AN EXCELLENT EXCHANGE OF TWO
PEOPLE THAT LOVE AND HONOR JESUS
TOGETHER. THE COMBINATION OF TWO
PEOPLE GETTING TOGETHER IN ONENESS.

AN ACT OF INTIMACY. SEX IS AN ACT OF
GOD'S LOVE. SATAN AND HIS DEMONS
HATE THE PURE IDEAS OF GOD.

THEREFORE, HE TURNED 1/3 OF THE
ANGELS AGAINST GOD. HE IS JEALOUS OF
GOD AND YOU. YOU BELONG TO THE
LORD, AND SATAN HATES EVERYTHING
THAT GOD HAS PREPARED FOR YOUR
PLEASURE.

SATAN DOES NOT LIKE THE ENJOYMENT
OF THE SAINTS (CHILDREN OF GOD).

1ST TIM 6:17 SAYS GOD GIVES YOU ALL THINGS TO RICHLY ENJOY. THIS VERY STATEMENT TORMENTS SATAN.
THIS IS WHY HE TRIES TO GET YOU DISTRACTED SO YOU WOULD NOT ENJOY WHAT GOD INTENDED TO BRING YOU TRUE PLEASURE.

SEXUAL THOUGHTS IS SOMETHING SATAN HAS USED TO CRIPPLE PEOPLE THAT HAVE A BIG DESTINY. IT HAS BECOME ONE OF HIS MAIN WEAPONS OF MASS DESTRUCTION. IT IS A SILENT KILLER THAT MANY NEVER DISCUSS WITH ANYBODY.

A SECRET ADDICTION!
A SECRET STRUGGLE!

A SHAMEFUL PLACE OF DEADLY FASCINATIONS.

LUST IS A COUNTERFEIT OF WORSHIP.

SATAN OFTEN WORKS THROUGH SEXUAL THOUGHTS TO DAMAGE YOUR PASSION FOR GOD AND THE PEOPLE OF GOD.

"WORSHIP IS WHERE YOU IMAGINE INTIMACY WITH JESUS, BUT LUST IS WHERE YOU IMAGINE INTIMACY WITH SOMEONE ELSE."

"LUST CAME TO REPLACE WORSHIP IN YOUR LIFE, BUT WORSHIP CAME TO REPLACE LUST IN YOUR LIFE."

WORSHIP IS WAY STRONGER THAN LUST, BUT IT IS MORE CHALLENGING TO PRODUCE.

IT TAKES DETERMINATION AND DISCIPLINE TO WORSHIP...BUT IT TAKES LAZINESS AND PRAYERLESSNESS TO LUST.

LUST CAN AUTOMATICALLY FLOW WHEN YOU ARE OUT OF WORSHIP... BUT TO STOP LUST YOU MUST BE INTENTIONAL, TARGET THAT SPIRIT, TO CRUSH IT AND SILENCE IT. SEXUAL THOUGHTS WILL ATTACK YOUR MIND WHEN YOU GET LAZY IN SPENDING TIME WITH GOD AND HIS WORD. THE DEMONS OF LUST AND SEXUAL WICKEDNESS HAVE DOORS TO ENTER YOUR MIND WHEN YOU DO NOT CONTINUALLY PRAY AND WORSHIP.

SEXUAL THOUGHTS ARE LIDS. THROUGH SEXUAL THOUGHTS DEMONS CAN PUT LIDS ON YOUR FINANCES SO THAT YOU NEVER PROSPER. DEMONS USE SEXUAL THOUGHTS

TO KEEP THE HEAVENS CLOSED OVER YOUR LIFE. LUST CLOSES THE HEAVENS OVER YOUR LIFE. THEREFORE, WHEN DAVID HAD LUST FOR BATHSHEBA HE ENTERED A BRIEF PERIOD WHEN THE HEAVENS WAS SHUT OVER HIS LIFE.

HE FASTED AND PRAYED FOR THE BABY TO LIVE, BUT GOD DID NOT LISTEN TO HIS PRAYER. GOD DID NOT RESPOND TO HIS FAST FOR THE BABY.

"FASTING WON'T WORK… WHEN YOUR MOTIVE FOR FASTING IS NOT RIGHT."

REMEMBER THE RELIGIOUS LEADERS FASTED BUT WERE STILL TRYING TO KILL JESUS. THE FAST THEY DID, WAS OUT OF PRIDE..BECAUSE THEY WERE STILL WICKED.

THE MOTIVE THEY HAD FOR FASTING WAS SELF RIGHTEOUSNESS.

THEY WANTED TO APPEAR TO BE MORE SPIRITUAL AND MORE RIGHTEOUS THAN EVERYONE ELSE.

THEY FASTED TO BE SEEN… WHICH WAS A WICKED MOTIVE.

MATTHEW 6:16-18 SAYS WHEN YOU FAST DO IT IN SECRET. DON'T LET ANYONE KNOW YOU ARE FASTING.

YOU MUST BE HUMBLE WITH THE WEAPONS GOD GIVES YOU. IF YOU'RE FASTING WHILE STILL PROUD YOU HAVE DEFEATED THE PURPOSE, THEREFORE YOUR FAST WILL NOT PRODUCE ANYTHING.

THEREFORE, THE HEAVENS WERE SHUT UP FOR DAVID.

WHEN WALKING IN LUST THE HEAVENS
WILL BEGIN TO SHUT OVER YOUR LIFE AND
THINGS WILL BEGIN DYING AROUND YOU.

YOUR RELATIONSHIP WITH JESUS WILL DIE.
YOUR FEAR OF GOD WILL DIE, SO DOES
YOUR PURITY AND INNOCENCE. IT IS MORE
FATAL THAN YOU KNOW.

"WHEN YOUR INTEGRITY DIES SO DOES
YOUR PEACE OF MIND."

SEXUAL THOUGHTS CAN BE IMPARTED TO
YOU BY BEING AROUND PERVERTED
PEOPLE. PEOPLE THAT ARE WILD IN THEIR
SEXUAL APPETITE CAN AFFECT YOU
MENTALLY. SOMETIMES THE REASON YOU
ARE STRUGGLING WITH SEXUAL THOUGHTS
IS BECAUSE OF WHO YOU HAVE MIXED

WITH. BE CAREFUL OF WHO YOU LET SPEAK INTO YOUR EARS. BE WISE WITH WHO YOU LET INTO YOUR LIFE.

PROVERBS 12:26 SAYS THE RIGHTEOUS MUST CHOOSE THEIR FRIENDS WISELY.

"WHAT YOU ARE AROUND… WILL ABOUND IN YOU."

YOU MUST GUARD YOUR HEART AND BE DEDICATED TO AVOIDING TRASH.

"DO NOT LET ANYONE PLANT GARBAGE ON YOUR GRACE… BUT USE YOUR GRACE TO AVOID GARBAGE."

"ANYONE WHO DOES NOT LIBERATE YOU IS STRENGTHENING YOUR BONDAGE."

"STAY AWAY FROM THOSE WHO THRILL YOUR FLESH... AND STAY CLOSE TO THOSE THAT KILL YOUR FLESH."

STUDY THE IMPARTATION THAT YOU RECEIVE FROM PEOPLE.

EVALUATE THE TRANSACTIONS THAT TAKE PLACE WHEN YOU CONVERSE WITH SOMEONE. THERE IS SOMETHING BEING RELEASED. IT CAN EITHER BE DEADLY OR HEAVENLY. ANYTIME YOU ARE DISTRACTED YOU ARE WEAK. WEAKNESS NEEDS YOU NEVER TO BE FOCUSED. WEAKNESS NEEDS YOU TO SET GOALS AND NEVER COMPLETE THEM. WEAKNESS NEEDS YOU TO GET TOO CASUAL WITH THE PRESENCE OF GOD IN YOUR LIFE, TO THE DEGREE WHERE YOU DO NOT PROTECT YOURSELF FROM PEOPLE AND THINGS

THAT WILL MAKE YOU FALL.

"WEAKNESS FEEDS OFF... YOU NOT FEEDING YOUR SPIRIT."

THE FLESH KNOWS WHEN YOU ARE NOT INVESTING IN PRAYER AND YOU ARE BECOMING A VICTIM OF PRAYERLESSNESS. WHENEVER YOU STOP CHASING AFTER GOD IT BRINGS FORTH CURSES IN YOUR THOUGHT LIFE. ANY DAY YOU DO NOT SEEK GOD THERE IS A DOOR OPEN TO THE DEMONIC REALM.

SEXUAL THOUGHTS CAN DOMINATE YOU THROUGH A RELATIONSHIP YOU HAD WITH SOMEONE OF YOUR PAST. YOU CAN CARRY TIES TO THEM IN YOUR SOUL, BECAUSE YOU ONCE WERE SEXUALLY ENGAGED WITH THEM. OLD RELATIONSHIPS CAN BE

SNEAKILY OPERATING IN YOU AND KEEPING YOU IN PRISON TO CERTAIN STRONGHOLDS IN YOUR MIND SEXUALLY.

SURRENDERING TO JESUS AND HIS WILL BREAKS THE SOUL TIE. WHEN YOU START TO GIVE JESUS YOUR UNDIVIDED ATTENTION, THAT IS WHEN YOU BEGIN TO OPERATE AUTHORITY OVER SOUL TIES, AND SEXUAL ADDICTIONS. THERE IS A CYCLE THAT SEXUAL THOUGHTS TRY TO PRODUCE IN YOU.

A PATTERN WHERE YOU KEEP GOING BACK TO THINGS THAT ARE SEXUALLY ENSLAVING YOU. IT MAY BE PORNOGRAPHY, MASTURBATION, OR FORNICATION. EVERY TIME YOU ARE MAKING STEPS TOWARDS BEING FAITHFUL TO GOD AND LIVING FOR HIM, THE DEVIL

TRIES TO PULL YOU BACK IN.

THE PROPHET OF GOD WILL ALWAYS BE
SENT IN THE TIME WHEN YOU ARE
STRUGGLING MENTALLY, AND THAT
PROPHET WILL BREAK THAT DEMON OFF
YOU OF WRONG THOUGHTS AND SOUL
TIES.
THE GLORY ON A PROPHET IS GREATER
AND STRONGER THAN ANY EVIL SPIRIT
THAT WILL TRY TO FIGHT YOU MENTALLY
AND EMOTIONALLY.

A PROPHET OF GOD WILL ALSO COVER YOU
FROM MENTAL BATTLES.

ANY DEMON THAT TORMENTS YOU WILL
DIE UNDER THE GLORY OF A PROPHET.

THE ANOINTING IS UPON YOU RIGHT NOW

TO ERADICATE THIS DEMONIC CYCLE. YOU WILL NOT GO BACK TO BEING A SEX SLAVE! THE DEVIL WILL NOT INFLUENCE YOU TO WATCH OR DO THINGS THAT ARE GOING TO PUSH YOU FURTHER AWAY FROM GODLINESS AND CLEAN THOUGHTS!

"GODLY GOALS… PRODUCES HOLINESS."

SET GOALS FOR YOURSELF OF WHAT YOU WANT TO BECOME THROUGH JESUS, AND WHAT YOU WANT TO DO FOR JESUS.

"SET SPIRITUAL GOALS… TO COME OUT OF FLESHLY STRONGHOLDS."

SPIRITUAL GOALS GIVE GRACE TO YOU WHILE YOU ARE BEING TEMPTED. WHILE YOU ARE EXPERIENCING THE VOICE OF YOUR FLESH SPEAKING TO YOU, GOD CAN

SPEAK TO YOU THROUGH SPIRITUAL GOALS. IF YOU DO NOT HAVE ANYTHING YOU WANT TO ACHIEVE IN CHRIST, YOU CAN BECOME AN EASY PREY FOR SEXUAL THOUGHTS AND SIN.

THERE IS ANOTHER STRATEGY SATAN USES TO BIRTH SEXUAL THOUGHTS IN YOU... THAT IS IN THE SEASON WHERE NOTHING IS GOING RIGHT, AND ALL HELL IS BREAKING LOOSE. THE DEVIL WILL USE DARK TIMES TO ENCOURAGE YOU TO GIVE INTO THE LUST OF YOUR FLESH.

"THE DEVIL... USES THE STORM TO DEFORM YOU. . . JESUS USES THE STORM TO TRANSFORM YOU."

THIS IS PART OF YOUR PROCESS. DO NOT LET TIMES WHEN THINGS ARE NOT GOING

YOUR WAY, CAUSE YOU TO START
CONSIDERING SOMETHING GOD SAYS NO
TO. KEEP PRESSING TOWARD THE
PROMISES GOD HAS FOR YOU. ALSO, DO
NOT LET THE DEVIL BULLY YOU WHILE
YOU ARE SINGLE. THIS IS A TIME WHERE
YOU MUST PRAY, FAST AND DIE TO
YOURSELF. REALLY BE SERIOUS ABOUT
KILLING YOUR FLESH WHILE BEING
SINGLE.

1ST CORINTHIANS 7:34 SAYS AN UNMARRIED
WOMAN CARES FOR THE THINGS OF THE
LORD, AND HOW SHE MAY PLEASE THE
LORD.

SO, WHEN YOU ARE NOT MARRIED, USE
THAT TIME TO BE VERY INTIMATE WITH
JESUS SPIRITUALLY, MENTALLY, AND
EMOTIONALLY. THIS IS A TIME OF STRONG

CONSECRATION AND WORSHIP. ROMANS 12:1 SAYS PRESENT YOUR BODY AS A LIVING SACRIFICE, HOLY, AND ACCEPTABLE TO GOD, WHICH IS YOUR REASONABLE SERVICE. SO, WHEN YOU ARE UNMARRIED THIS IS THE BEST TIME TO START SACRIFICING YOUR BODY UNTO THE LORD. GIVE HIM YOUR BODY, YOUR FEELINGS, YOUR DESIRES, AND ALL YOUR SENSES. GALATIANS 5:24 SAYS THOSE THAT BELONG TO CHRIST, HAVE CRUCIFIED THE FLESH, WITH ALL OF IT'S PASSIONS AND LUST. SO, THIS IS A REALM WHEN YOU BELONG TO JESUS AND HIS POWER, YOU CRUCIFY YOUR FLESH, AND YOUR PASSIONS. YOU LAY THEM ASIDE. HEBREWS 12:1 SAYS LAYING ASIDE EVERY WEIGHT, AND THE SIN THAT SO EASILY BESET US.

"YOU MUST GET RID OF... WHAT IS TRYING

TO GET RID OF YOU."

IT IS YOUR JOB TO SILENCE YOUR FLESH, SO YOU CAN HEAR GOD. YOU DO THIS BY RENEWING YOUR MIND. YOUR SOUL IS YOUR MIND WILL AND EMOTIONS. THESE ARE YOUR SENSES. YOUR SENSES WILL ALWAYS BE INACCURATE WHEN YOU'RE NOT IN THE PRESENCE OF GOD. YOUR FLESH DOES NOT NEED TO BE ACTIVATED BUT YOUR SPIRIT DOES.

THAT'S WHY DAVID SAID *"QUICKEN ME BY YOUR WORD." PSALM 119:107.*

YOUR FLESH IS ALREADY ACTIVATED WHEN YOU'RE NOT IN THE WORD.

YOU SILENCE YOUR FLESH JUST BY WALKING IN THE SPIRIT. MANY BELIEVE

FASTING SILENCES YOUR FLESH, BUT
FASTING ONLY PREPARES YOUR FLESH TO
BE SILENCED.

EPHESIANS 4:27 SAYS GIVE NO PLACE TO
THE DEVIL.

YOUR MIND IS NOT A DWELLING PLACE
FOR DEMONS. THEREFORE, YOU MUST
BECOME AGGRESSIVE IN THE
PRESERVATION OF YOUR MIND.

"KEEP IT SANCTIFIED... FROM THE DEVIL'S
LIES."

PLEAD THE BLOOD OF JESUS OVER YOUR
MIND DAILY.

BE VERY CONSISTENT IN THINKING
THOUGHTS THAT ARE FROM MEDITATING

ON THE WORD OF GOD.

HOPE IS...
AN ANOINTING THAT MAKES YOUR MIND
GO FORWARD WITH JESUS.

STAY AWAY FROM WHATEVER STOPS THE
MOMENTUM OF YOUR LIBERTY. STAY IN
FREEDOM AND LIBERTY.
CHOOSE THE JOY OF YOUR SALVATION.

PSALM 51:12 SAYS RESTORE TO ME THE JOY
OF MY SALVATION.

"JOY EMPOWERS YOU... OVER THE SINFUL
NATURE."

ENJOY THOUGHTS OF WHAT JESUS HAS
DONE FOR YOU.
THINK ABOUT HOW JESUS DIED FOR YOU,

AND ROSE TO GIVE YOU EVERYTHING YOU
DESIRE.

KEEP YOUR MIND STAYED ON DIVINE
THINGS THAT KEEP YOUR ANOINTING
INSPIRED AND OVERFLOWING.

V CHAPTER: HOW JESUS MANIFEST

MANY DO NOT KNOW HOW TO UNLOCK
JESUS.

UNLOCKING JESUS… IS THE ABILITY TO
MAKE HIM PLEASED, HAPPY, INSPIRED, AND
SATISFIED.

YOU UNLOCK JESUS IN YOUR LIFE WHEN
YOU SERVE A MAN OF GOD.

YOU UNLOCK JESUS WHEN YOU HONOR
YOUR DIVINE CONNECTION.

IF YOU TREAT SOMEONE THAT IS DIVINELY
SENT TO YOUR LIFE WITH LOVE, IT
UNLOCKS JESUS. THE ANOINTING BEGINS
TO INTENSIFY IN YOU.

JESUS HIMSELF SAID "I AM THE DOOR" IN JOHN 10:9.

A DOOR CAN EITHER BE CLOSED OR OPENED, LOCKED, OR UNLOCKED.

YOUR DECISIONS TO PURSUE JESUS INCREASES YOUR FOCUS.

"YOUR ANOINTING… WILL NEVER BE STRONGER THAN YOUR FOCUS."

WHENEVER JESUS SPEAKS TO YOU OR ASSIGNS YOU TO DO ANYTHING, THERE WILL BE MANY DISTRACTIONS.

WHEN THE LORD STARTS PULLING YOU IN, THE DEVIL STARTS PULLING YOU AWAY. DISTRACTION IS A DEMONIC FOCUS WHERE YOUR THOUGHTS GET CAUGHT.

CAUGHT IN VANITY.

CAUGHT IN SIN.

CAUGHT IN DECEPTION.

CAUGHT IN WEAKNESS.

"VAIN IMAGINATION PRODUCES
STAGNATION."

WHATEVER SLOWS YOU DOWN IS ANTI-GOD.
NOTHING THAT COMES FROM GOD, SLOWS
YOU DOWN.

"DEMONS WORK THROUGH
DISTRACTIONS… GOD WORK THROUGH
ATTRACTIONS."

GOD CAN USE A HANDSOME MAN OR
BEAUTIFUL WOMAN TO ATTRACT YOU TO
HIM. MANY HAVE BECOME SAVED
THROUGH MY MINISTRY BECAUSE MY LOOK
ATTRACTED THEM. FOR MOSES, IT WAS A

BURNING BUSH. FOR THE PROSTITUTES, IT WAS JESUS MERCY THAT DREW THEM TOWARDS GOD.

"WHEN YOU NEGLECT PRAYER, YOU ACCEPT STRUGGLE."

"WHEN YOU REJECT WORSHIP, YOU RESURRECT WEAKNESS."

"YOUR MIND CRAVES THE BEHIND & NOT THE DIVINE."

YOUR MIND CRAVES: REBELLION, WORRY, FEAR, BITTERNESS, PROCRASTINATION, AND WITCHCRAFT. THESE ARE ALL SNEAKY FORMS OF REBELLION. THEY FEED THE DEMON OF CONDEMNATION. YOUR MIND LOVES THE PAST. YOUR MIND WILL CONDEMN YOU. GOD CAN FORGIVE YOUR

SINS, BUT CONDEMNATION WILL KEEP YOU FROM FORGIVING YOURSELF. DO NOT BECOME YOUR OWN ENEMY. FIGHTING AGAINST YOURSELF, AS SATAN SMOOTHLY DECEIVES YOUR MIND INTO A WRONG FOCUS. HE CAN PLAY WITH IT, AND SEDUCE IT INTO DISAGREEMENT WITH GOD'S WORD. YOUR MIND CARRIES A FRAGRANCE; EITHER THE DEAD PLACES OF YOUR PAST OR THE UNFAMILIAR PLACES OF YOUR FUTURE.

"DISTRACTION IS . . . THE MOTIVE OF SATAN."

DEMONS ARE THE CO-WORKERS AND THE EMPLOYEES OF SATAN.
DEMONS MOVE IN: RANKS, GROUPS, AND CLIQUES. THEY HAVE STRATEGIES, PLANS, AND ASSIGNMENTS. THE MAJOR

ASSIGNMENT OF A DEMON IS TO BLIND YOU. BLINDNESS IS THE MINISTRY OF AN EVIL SPIRIT. THE ROOT OF ALL STAGNATION AND CURSES IS BLINDNESS. PEOPLE CANNOT MOVE WITH GOD, OBEY GOD OR COME OUT OF HARDSHIP, NOR BAD DECISIONS BECAUSE OF BLINDNESS. BLINDNESS IS A HOLY SPIRIT QUENCHER. IT QUENCHES THE HOLY SPIRIT AND INCREASES CONFUSION.

CONFUSION IS WHERE DEMONS COUNTERFEIT THE VOICE OF GOD, TO DESTROY YOUR CONFIDENCE IN HIS VOICE.

JAMES 1:8 SAYS "A DOUBLE MINDED MAN IS UNSTABLE IN ALL HIS WAYS."

"A DOUBLE MINDED MAN IS A DOUBLE BLINDED MAN."

ELIJAH THE PROPHET RELEASED A DOUBLE PORTION UPON ELISHA FOR HIM TO SEE IN *2 KINGS 2:13*... BUT, DEMONS DO THE OPPOSITE. WHICH IS GIVE YOU A DOUBLE PORTION OF BLINDNESS.

LUKE 4:18 THE SPIRIT OF THE LORD WAS UPON JESUS "FOR THE RECOVERY OF SIGHT."

SATAN IS THE SPIRIT OF BLINDNESS. HIS IMPARTATION OF BLINDNESS CAME UPON THE WOMAN IN THE GARDEN OF EDEN. THEN THE WOMAN TRANSFERRED THAT DEMON OF BLINDNESS TO ADAM. THEN ADAM TRANSFERRED THAT DEMON OF BLINDNESS TO HIS SON CAIN.

THIS IS THE FIRST MURDER SCENE ON EARTH. WHEN CAIN KILLED HIS BROTHER ABEL, GOD CONFRONTED HIM AND CAIN

REPLIED, *"AM I MY BROTHER'S KEEPER?"* **IN**
GENESIS 4:9 CAIN DID NOT BELIEVE THAT HE
WAS WRONG FOR KILLING HIS BROTHER
BECAUSE THE DEMON OF BLINDNESS WAS
UPON HIM. HE ALSO DID NOT TAKE
RESPONSIBILITY FOR KILLING HIS BROTHER
BECAUSE OF THIS DEMON.

"BLINDNESS DAMAGES YOUR
ACCOUNTABILITY."

THIS EVIL SPIRIT WILL CONVINCE YOU
THAT YOU ARE RIGHT, EVEN WHEN THE
HOLY SPIRIT IS CONVINCING YOU THAT YOU
ARE WRONG.
JESUS REINSTALLED SIGHT TO YOUR SPIRIT.
THE NEW DISPENSATION OF THE
PROPHETIC. THE PROPHETIC IS JESUS
SUPPLYING GRACE TO WEAK VISION. THERE
ARE IMPARTATIONS THAT JESUS RELEASES

TO STRENGTHEN YOUR SIGHT SYSTEM.

"WITHOUT SIGHT. . . SIN WILL DOMINATE."

"SIGHTLESSNESS . . . THIS INCREASES
INACCURACY WITH GOD."
"IN SIGHT . . . COMES FROM THE HOLY SPIRIT
WITHIN."

PROTECT THAT SIGHT! SPENDING TIME
WITH JESUS CAN INTENSIFY YOUR SIGHT
AND BRING IT TO ANOTHER LEVEL. GOD
TRUSTS YOU WITH MORE INSIGHT WHEN HE
SEES YOUR DISCIPLINE. FASTING AND
PRAYING INCREASES THE PROPHETIC
BECAUSE IT SHOWS DISCIPLINE.

WHENEVER YOU SHOW MATURITY, YOU
ALLOW GOD TO POUR THE OIL OF THE
PROPHETIC ON YOU

"MATURITY IS . . . A DECISION TO ALLOW
GOD TO PROMOTE YOU.
DISCIPLINE IS... A DECISION TO ALLOW GOD
TO PREPARE YOU."

MATURITY DECIDES A PROPHET'S LEVEL.

I CORINTHIANS 13:11 SAYS "WHEN I WAS A CHILD, I
SPOKE LIKE A CHILD; I UNDERSTOOD AS A CHILD, I
THOUGHT AS A CHILD, BUT WHEN I BECAME A MAN I
PUT CHILDISH THINGS AWAY."

THE LACK OF MATURITY WILL DAMAGE A
PROPHET'S GIFT AND CAUSE INACCURACY.
THE VOICE OF GOD WILL BE DIM TO YOUR
SPIRIT. LACK OF MATURITY WILL ALSO
ATTRACT UNNECESSARY ATTACKS ON YOUR
LIFE. IMMATURITY INCREASES FLAWS.
JONAH HEARD GOD TELL HIM TO GO TO
NINEVEH, BUT HE DISOBEYED. HE WAS

IMMATURE. HE HAD FLAWS. THEN GOD SAVED NINEVEH THROUGH THE MINISTRY OF PROPHET JONAH.

HE GETS VERY ANGRY IN *JONAH 4:2-4*. HE WAS AN IMMATURE PROPHET, THEREFORE HE WALKED IN FLAWS, REBELLION AND BITTERNESS.

JESUS DOES NOT LIKE WHEN YOU FIGHT THE PROPHETIC CALLING OR ASSIGNMENT ON YOUR LIFE. OBEDIENCE IS ALWAYS BETTER THAN SACRIFICE. IMMATURITY FIGHTS AGAINST GOD AND HIS WILL FOR YOUR LIFE.

"MATURITY IS OBEDIENCE WITHOUT EMOTIONAL SUPPORT."
YOU RECEIVE PROMOTION WHEN YOU OBEY GOD WITHOUT YOUR FEELINGS.

"DO NOT LET YOUR FEELINGS LEAD YOU...
LEAD YOUR FEELINGS."

THE REALM OF FEELINGS IS THE REALM OF
DEFEAT.

"WORSHIP UNLOCKS JESUS... DENYING
YOURSELF IS THE FIRST STAGE OF
ACCESSING GOD."

ONCE YOU DENY YOURSELF AND TAKE
YOUR EYES OFF YOU, IS WHEN JESUS CAN
MANIFEST HIMSELF.

"DISCIPLINE INCREASES DIVINE
ENCOUNTERS."
DISCIPLINE IS A SEASON THAT COMES
BEFORE PROMOTION. GOD WILL NOT LIFT
YOU UP UNTIL YOU LOWER YOURSELF.

"IF YOU ARE HUMBLE... YOU WILL NOT STUMBLE."

HUMILITY GIVES YOU THE GO AHEAD TO HELP YOU GROW AHEAD.

PROMOTION REQUIRES YOU TO EMPTY YOURSELF OF YOUR OWN AGENDA.

"GOD REQUIRES DILIGENCE... NOT ARROGANCE."

ARROGANCE IS A SATANIC ARROW. IT IS A SATANIC WEAPON THAT REFUSES GOD'S CORRECTION OR WISDOM TO TEACH YOU.

RIGHTEOUSNESS ATTRACTS PROMOTION. TEACHABILITY ATTRACTS FAVOR.

WHEN YOU BEHAVE HOW GOD WANTS YOU TO BEHAVE, SAY WHAT GOD WANTS YOU TO SAY, DO WHAT GOD WANTS YOU TO DO, AND BE WHO GOD WANTS YOU TO BE IS WHEN YOU WILL SEE PROMOTION.

PROVERBS 29:25 "THE FEAR OF MAN BRINGS YOU A SNARE."

IF YOU FEAR PEOPLE, YOU CANNOT PLEASE JESUS IN THIS LIFE. THE FEAR OF MAN WILL BLOCK YOU FROM WALKING IN RIGHTEOUSNESS, THROUGH INTIMIDATION.

YOU WILL END UP IGNORING WHAT GOD SAID AND DELAY HIS DIVINE INSTRUCTIONS.
WHEN YOU WORSHIP, THERE ARE WORSHIPING ANGELS WORSHIPING WITH YOU.

THAT IS WHY THE PRESENCE OF GOD
BECOMES SO TANGIBLE AND REAL IN
WORSHIP, BECAUSE ANGELS JOIN IN WITH
YOU AND THEY CARRY THE VERY SAME
ATMOSPHERE OF GOD.

IT IS IMPORTANT THAT YOU TAKE TIME TO
WORSHIP JESUS, IF NOT, DEMON SPIRITS
WILL BEGIN TO IMPART WRONG THOUGHTS
IN YOUR MIND AND HEART.

"WORSHIP PURGES. . . YOUR URGES."

"WORSHIP IS…THE RECEPTIVITY OF GOD'S
INSTRUCTIONS."

"WORSHIP…MATURES…FAITH."

WORSHIP IS…KNOWING WHAT WORDS TO
SAY TO A MAN OF GOD.

WORSHIP IS…KNOWING HOW TO RESPOND TO DIVINE PRESENCE.

WORSHIP IS…AGREEMENT WITH GOD'S DECISIONS.

WORSHIP IS…PROTECTED THROUGH SANCTIFICATION.

BEFORE YOU CAN BE A TRUE WORSHIPPER YOU WILL HAVE TO CONSISTENTLY SHUT DOWN ACCESS TO PEOPLE WHO ARE NOT RESPECTFUL TO THE HOLY SPIRIT.

WHOEVER IS CLOSE TO YOU CAN INFLUENCE YOU THE MOST.

THOSE CLOSEST HAVE THE GREATEST IMPACT ON YOU. EITHER FOR BETTER OR FOR WORSE.

"WHOEVER HAS YOUR FOCUS. . . WILL FRAME YOUR MIND."

"WORSHIP ANOINTS YOU TO STOP GIVING WRONG PEOPLE ACCESS."

THE PRESENCE OF GOD VACUUMS THE DUST FROM THINGS THAT ARE OLD AND FORBIDDEN OUT OF YOUR LIFE.

"OLD THINGS HAVE PASSED AWAY BEHOLD, ALL THINGS ARE BECOME NEW" – II CORINTHIANS 5:17.

WORSHIP RENEWS YOUR MIND AND FOCUS TO WALK IN THAT NEWNESS.
WORSHIP INSPIRES YOUR PASSION FOR GOD.

Prophetic Mysteries

VI CHAPTER:

PROPHETIC SIGNALS

GOD SPEAKS…WHEN YOU ARE HUNGRY.

GOD SPEAKS…WHEN YOU ARE ATTENTIVE.

GOD SPEAKS…WHEN YOU ARE CALLED.

GOD SPEAKS…WHEN YOU ARE CHOSEN.

GOD SPEAKS…WHEN YOU ARE FOCUSED.

GOD SPEAKS…WHEN YOU ARE HATED.

GOD SPEAKS…WHEN YOU ARE HURTING.

GOD SPEAKS…WHEN YOU ARE LONELY.

GOD SPEAKS…WHEN YOU ARE CONFUSED.

GOD SPEAKS…WHEN YOU ARE RESTLESS.

GOD SPEAKS…WHEN YOU ARE ABUSED.

GOD SPEAKS…WHEN YOU ARE WEARY.

GOD SPEAKS…WHEN YOU ARE JOYFUL.

GOD SPEAKS…WHEN YOU ARE STRESSED.

GOD SPEAKS…WHEN YOU ARE HAPPY.

GOD SPEAKS…WHEN YOU ARE LOST.

GOD SPEAKS…WHEN YOU ARE FEARFUL.

GOD SPEAKS…WHEN YOU ARE SEARCHING.

GOD SPEAKS…WHEN YOU ARE
DISTRACTED.

YOU WILL NEVER HEAR HIM…UNTIL YOU BE
STILL.

"STILLNESS INVITES… GOD'S REALNESS."

"STILLNESS INVITES…REVELATION."

"STILLNESS INVITES…WISDOM AND ANGELS."

"STILLNESS IS…MY WAITING ROOM TO RECEIVE A VISITATION FROM GOD."

"STILLNESS CREATES… MY APPOINTMENT WITH JESUS."

"STILLNESS IS…YIELDING TO GOD'S TIMING."

"STILLNESS PERFECTS…MY INTIMACY WITH JESUS."

"STILLNESS POSITIONS ME… TO RECEIVE WHAT GOD IS SAYING NEXT."

"STILLNESS ADDS PASSION…TO MY

INTIMACY WITH JESUS."

DISRESPECT DESTROYS INTIMACY. THIS APPLIES TO MARRIAGE AND RELATIONSHIPS, BUT MORE IMPORTANTLY THIS APPLIES TO YOUR RELATIONSHIP WITH JESUS THROUGH HIS HOLY SPIRIT.

DISCIPLINE YOURSELF, SO YOU DO NOT DISRESPECT THE HOLY GHOST.

DISRESPECT DESTROYS INTIMACY...BUT WORSHIP AND SENSITIVITY RESTORES INTIMACY.

"HONOR RESTORES INTIMACY WITH JESUS." HONOR IS CORRECTING WHAT MAKES GOD DISPLEASED.

"HONOR BIRTHS... GOD'S PLEASURE."

"HONOR IS…A DOOR TO GOD'S HEART."

"DISRESPECTING JESUS . . . IS NEGLECTING JESUS." *PROVERBS 3:5 "ACKNOWLEDGE THE LORD IN ALL YOUR WAYS AND HE SHALL DIRECT YOUR PATH."*

WHEN YOU BEGIN TO MOVE IN A SPIRIT OF DISRESPECT, IT DAMAGES THE STRENGTH OF GOD IN YOUR HEART AND MIND.

THE DANGEROUS SIDE EFFECT OF THIS IS SLOWLY BUT SURELY YOU WILL SLIDE BACK INTO THE DEMONIC REALM WHERE EVIL SPIRITS WILL DOMINATE YOUR MEMORY.

"YOUR MEMORY…DECIDES YOUR PRESENT FOCUS."

"YOUR PRESENT FOCUS…DECIDES YOUR

PRESENT DECISIONS."

"YOUR PRESENT DECISIONS...DECIDES THE KIND OF FUTURE GOD CAN GET TO YOU."

THE PAST WILL NEVER PASS FROM YOU. THE EVIL SPIRITS WILL KEEP BRINGING IT UP. BITTERNESS WILL RULE YOU. YOU WILL BLAME OTHERS FOR YOUR CONDITIONS IN LIFE. YOU WILL ALSO BE IMMATURE AND NEVER TAKE RESPONSIBILITY FOR YOUR LIFE.

WHEN YOU MOVE IN A SPIRIT OF DISRESPECTING JESUS, AND NOT ASKING JESUS WHAT TO DO IN YOUR DAILY DECISIONS...DOORS WILL BEGIN TO OPEN FOR UNCLEAN SPIRITS IN YOUR LIFE.

THESE UNCLEAN SPIRITS WILL BRING YOU

BACK INTO FILTHY AND TOXIC DESIRES. YOU WILL CRAVE LAWLESSNESS WHICH IS SIN. YOUR FLESH WILL BE OUT OF CONTROL.

SOMETIMES YOU WILL BEGIN TO DESIRE SEX WHICH CAN LEAD YOU INTO OPENING DOORS TO PEOPLE THAT GOD HAS SHUT OFF FROM YOUR PRESENT AND FUTURE.

WHEN YOU DESTROY INTIMACY WITH JESUS, IT CAUSES YOU TO LOSE YOUR LIBERTY. LIBERTY CAN BE LOST, ESPECIALLY IF YOU DO NOT FOLLOW THROUGH WITH WHAT GOD TOLD YOU TO DO TO STAY SAFE. IN THE BOOK OF GENESIS, ADAM LOST HIS LIBERTY BECAUSE HE DID NOT FOLLOW THROUGH WITH INSTRUCTIONS. IN THE BOOK OF *JUDGES 16* SAMSON LOST HIS LIBERTY BECAUSE HE DID NOT FOLLOW THROUGH WITH INSTRUCTIONS.

"DISCRETION IS . . . WHERE YOU CHOOSE TO SUBMIT TO GOD'S GUIDANCE THAT PROTECTS YOU."

PROPHETIC SIGNALS CAN WORK THROUGH A FEELING. GOD WILL LET YOU KNOW WHO IS A SNAKE OR SUSPECT IN YOUR LIFE. JESUS LETS YOU FEEL A WEIRD FEELING ABOUT A PERSON. DO NOT IGNORE THAT! IT IS DIVINE SUSPICION.

"THE SNAKES ARE THE FAKES IN YOUR LIFE."
WHEN YOU IGNORE JESUS AND BECOME GUILTY OF NOT FELLOWSHIPPING WITH HIM IT INCREASES YOUR BLINDNESS AND CANCELS YOUR DISCERNMENT.

"WHEN YOU LACK MINDFULNESS OF CHRIST

IT ENHANCES BLINDNESS IN YOUR LIFE."

STAY IN THE MODE OF LISTENING AND ATTENTIVENESS. DO NOT BECOME SLUGGISH AND LAZY WHEN IT COMES TO YOUR STREAM. YOUR STREAM IS THE WAY THE HOLY SPIRIT FLOWS THROUGH YOU. MORDECAI WAS THE ONLY ONE WHO DID NOT BOW TO HAMAN. MORDECAI WAS THE ONLY ONE OPERATING IN PROPHETIC SIGNALS. A MAJOR PROPHETIC ANOINTING WAS UPON MORDECAI; TO THE EXTENT HE IMPARTED WISDOM AND DISCERNMENT TO QUEEN ESTHER. HE LET ESTHER KNOW HOW TO EXPOSE HAMAN AND HIS PLOT TO DESTROY THE JEWS. ALL BECAUSE MORDECAI YIELDED TO THE PROPHETIC SIGNALS. HE SAW WHAT GOD SAW.

PROPHETIC SIGNALS IS GOD IMPARTING

AND IMPLANTING HIS POINT OF VIEW.

PROPHETIC SIGNALS WORK THROUGH
EMPTINESS. WHEN YOU FEEL EMPTY
SPIRITUALLY, MEANING NO ANOINTING, NO
FOCUS, AND NO STEADY PRAYER LIFE, GOD
IS SPEAKING TO YOU.

"EMPTINESS MEANS…THERE IS A
IMPARTATION FROM A MAN OF GOD
AWAITING YOU."

"EMPTINESS QUICKENS YOUR SPIRIT."
"EMPTINESSS CONVICTS YOU OF THE NEXT
LEVEL IN GOD, YOU SHOULD BE PURSUING.

"EMPTINESS REVEALS…WHAT IS DRAINING
YOU."

"EMPTINESS REVEALS…WHAT WRONG

THOUGHTS YOU MUST CONQUER."

"EMPTINESS REVEALS WHO, WHAT, AND WHERE IS HINDERING YOUR ANOINTING."

THIS IS HOW YOU DISCERN A PROPHETIC SIGNAL THAT SOMEONE IS A PARASITE TO YOUR LIFE. SUFFOCATING THE LIFE OF GOD OUT OF YOU. THERE ARE PEOPLE THAT CAN EITHER SUCK THE LIFE OF GOD OUT OF YOU OR AWAY FROM YOU. THIS MEANS YOU HAD FELLOWSHIP WITH JESUS AND THEY DISTRACTED YOU. IF THEY SUCK HIS LIFE AWAY FROM YOU THIS MEANS THEY WERE SENT FOR YOU TO NEVER HAVE ANY FORM OF FRIENDSHIP WITH JESUS. EVEN FRUSTRATION IS A PROPHETIC SIGNAL THAT GOD WANTS TO BRING TREMENDOUS CHANGE TO YOUR EXPERIENCE WITH HIM.

HOW DEMONS RULE WHERE THERE IS NO PROPHETIC COVERING OVER YOUR LIFE

PEOPLE THAT ARE SENT BY SATAN WILL ALWAYS TALK ABOUT YOUR PAST, BUT WHEN JESUS SENDS A PROPHET TO YOUR LIFE THEY WILL TALK ABOUT YOUR FUTURE. "THOSE WHO KEEP YOU IN YESTERDAY... CAN TAKE YOUR YES AWAY." "YOUR ZEAL TO OBEY JESUS CAN DIE IF YOU LISTEN TO A LIE." WHEN SOMEONE IS SUCCESSFUL IN GETTING YOU TO CONCENTRATE ON YOUR PAST, YOUR GROWTH AND SEASON WILL NEVER BEGIN TO ACCELERATE. "WHEN DEMONS TAKE OVER YOUR MIND... YOU WILL BE DISTRACTED ALWAYS LOOKING BEHIND." WHEN THE DEVIL SPEAKS TO YOU, YOU LOOK BACKWARDS. "WHEN GOD SPEAKS TO YOU, YOU WILL LOOK FORWARD." ANYONE WHO KEEPS YOU IN

THE PAST IS DANGEROUS TO YOUR PRESENT SEASON. THOSE THAT DIRECT YOUR FOCUS BACK TO OLD THINGS ARE A STUMBLING BLOCK TO YOUR PROPHETIC ANOINTING. PROPHETIC GRACE NOT ONLY EMPOWERS YOU TO PROPHESY TO OTHERS . . . BUT ALLOWS YOU TO COVER YOURSELF. "DEMONS ARE GIVING PLACE . . . WHERE THERE IS NO PROPHETIC GRACE." PROPHETIC GRACE IS WHEN JESUS IS SPEAKING TO YOU ABOUT YOUR FUTURE, BUT IMPARTING HIS POWER TO YOU IN THE PRESENT. . . SO YOU CAN GET THERE. *HEBREWS 12:2 "FOR THE JOY THAT WAS SET BEFORE HIM, JESUS ENDURED THE CROSS."*

Prophetic Mysteries

VII CHAPTER: HOW TO INCREASE TRANCES, DREAMS, VISIONS, OPEN VISIONS

EVERYTHING GOD DOES... CAN BE ACTIVATED. IT CAN BE TRIGGERED.

GOD CAN BE INSPIRED THROUGH YOUR FAITH. *MARK 5:34* JESUS SAID, *"YOUR*

FAITH HAS MADE YOU WHOLE."

GOD CAN BE INSPIRED BY WORSHIP. JESUS
WAS SILENT TO THE WOMAN OF CANAAN
WHOSE DAUGHTER WAS DEMON POSSESSED
BUT THE BIBLE SAID SHE WORSHIPPED HIM
MATTHEW 15:25.

TO INCREASE YOUR SIGHT IN YOUR
SPIRIT…YOU HAVE TO STOP DEPENDING
ON YOUR SIGHT IN THE FLESH.

THE NATURAL SIGHT IS THE LEAST WAY OF
SEEING.
GOD CREATED YOU TO SEE THROUGH YOUR
SPIRITUAL EYES. YOUR SPIRIT EYES CAN SEE
MORE ADVANCED AND IS THE ORIGINAL
WAY GOD WANTED YOU TO SEE.

MEDITATION IS THE KEY TO ACTIVATING

TRANCES, DREAMS, VISIONS, AND OPEN VISION. MEDITATION IS AN ANOINTING OF JESUS. *ISAIAH 26:3* TOLD US IF WE MEDITATE ON JESUS IT WILL BRING YOU INTO SUPERNATURAL PEACE. *JOSHUA 1:8* REVEALED TO YOU THAT MEDITATION CAN BRING YOU INTO SUPERNATURAL PROSPERITY.

"MEDITATION . . . IS DIVINE FOCUS."

IT IS AN ANOINTING TO STAY IN PRAYER, STAY IN FAITH, STAY IN WORSHIP, EVEN STAY IN FORGIVENESS TOWARDS OTHERS. MEDITATION DECIDES THE DEMONSTRATION OF THE PROPHETIC ON YOUR LIFE.

MEDITATION INCREASES YOUR ACCURACY PROPHETICALLY. WHEN YOU MEDITATE, YOU ZOOM IN ON GOD AND ZOOM OUT OF THE FLESH.

"IT ALLOWS YOU TO EXIT THE FLESH... INTO GOD'S BEST."

"PROPHECY IS… WHEN YOU LOCATE OTHERS

FAITH & MEDITATION...IS WHERE YOU LOCATE GOD."

WHEN YOU MEDITATE, YOUR SPIRIT IS SEARCHING FOR JESUS. SEARCHING FOR HIS PRESENCE.

THE SCRIPTURE SAID, **"CAN YOU BY SEARCHING FIND OUT GOD?" "CAN YOU FIND OUT THE ALMIGHTY?"** *JOB 11:7*

MATTHEW 7:7 "ASK AND IT SHALL BE GIVEN SEEK AND YE SHALL FIND.

"MEDITATION ALLOWS YOUR SPIRIT TO ACCURATELY SEEK JESUS."

IN THE GOSPELS, MARTHA SOUGHT JESUS THROUGH WORKS, MARY SOUGHT JESUS THROUGH WORSHIP. MARY WAS ATTENTIVE.

MEDITATION IS A DEEP, DEEP REALM OF WORSHIP. TO THE DEGREE, IF YOU ARE DEEP IN MEDITATION AND WORSHIP, YOU STEP INTO THE SUPERNATURAL MANTLE OF A SEER. YOUR SPIRIT EYES WILL OPEN. A TRANCE IS VERY SIMILAR TO AN OPEN VISION. THESE HAPPEN MOSTLY, WHEN YOU ARE AWAKE AND NOT SLEEP.

DEEP MEDITATION ON JESUS ALLOWS YOUR SPIRIT TO COME INTO THIS DEEP REALM OF SEEING. THIS INTENSIFIES THE PROPHETIC.

MANY HAVE NEVER ENTERED THIS GLORY ZONE, BECAUSE IT REQUIRES YOU TO BE

RESISTANT OF WRONG PEOPLE AND WRONG FOCUS. IT REQUIRES YOU TO CAST DOWN IMAGINATIONS THAT COME FROM EVIL SPIRITS THAT LOVE TO SEE YOU MISS GOD.

THIS DEEP PROPHETIC REALM OF SEEING IN THE SPIRIT WITH TRANCES AND OPEN VISION ARE AVAILABLE AND THE LORD JESUS WANTS TO GIVE IT TO YOU. GUARD YOUR HEART. *PROVERBS 4:23* REVEALED HOW TO COME INTO A STRONGER SEER ANOINTING.

YOU MUST GUARD YOUR HEART WITH ALL DILIGENCE, FOR OUT OF IT FLOWS THE ISSUES OF LIFE. THE LIFE OF THE PROPHETIC ANOINTING IS IN YOUR HEART SO GUARD IT WISELY.

"THE PROPHTEIC ANOINTING…FLOWS

WHEN YOU HONOR A PROPHET."

"THE PROPHETIC ANOINTING…FLOWS WHEN YOU IMITATE ELISHA…TO SERVE YOUR PROPHET."

"THE PROPHETIC ANOINTING…FLOWS WHEN YOU SOW INTO YOUR PROPHET. "THE PROPHETIC ANOINTING…STRENGTHENS WHEN YOU MEDITATE ON THE WORD OF GOD."

"THE PROPHETIC ANOINTING…GROWS."

"THE PROPHETIC ANOINTING…STRENGTHENS WHEN YOU SPEAK THE WORD OF GOD TO YOURSELF."

"THE PROPHETIC

ANOINTING…STRENGTHENS WHEN YOU
LEAVE EVERYTHING TO FOLLOW JESUS."

"THE PROPHETIC
ANOINTING…STRENGTHENS WHEN YOU
ASK GOD FOR IT."

"THE PROPHETIC
ANOINTING…STRENGTHENS WHEN YOU
PRAY IN THE SPIRIT MORE."

VIII CHAPTER: ENGAGING THE PRESENCE OF JESUS

"SILENCE YOUR DESIRES…UNTIL YOU DISCOVER WHAT JESUS DESIRES."

"CRAVING JESUS…IS PERSUADING JESUS TO FAVOR YOU."

"WHEN JESUS IS STANDING BEFORE YOU…NEVER BE TORMENTED BY THE PAST STANDING BEHIND YOU."

"THE PATH OF SELF DENIAL…IS THE PATH TO JESUS."

"YOU HAVE TO LEAVE "YOU" …TO RECEIVE WHAT GOD HAS FOR YOU."
"JESUS IS… HIDDEN IN A PROPHET.
JESUS IS… HIDDEN IN A DIVINE CONNECTION.
JESUS IS… HIDDEN IN A DIVINE INSTRUCTION."

"THE PURSUIT OF JESUS…REVEALS YOUR VIRTUE AS A WOMAN…IT REVEALS YOUR KINGSHIP AS A MAN."

"REAL QUEENS FACE JESUS."

"REAL KINGS CHASE JESUS."

"YOU HAVE TO DEFEAT THE PRINCE OF THE POWER OF THE AIR…BEFORE YOU CAN BE CLOSE TO THE PRINCE OF PEACE."

"EVERY INSTRUCTION TO LEAVE A WRONG PERSON…MAKES ROOM FOR GOD'S ENTRANCE."

"THOSE THAT DESIRE JESUS…INSPIRE JESUS."

"WORSHIP IS…WHEN YOU VALUE GOD IN AREAS THAT OTHERS DESPISE HIM."

"HONOR MOVES YOU TO DO SOMETHING TOWARDS JESUS…AND YOUR HONOR MOVES JESUS TO DO SOMETHING TOWARDS YOU."

"RECEPTIVITY ENERGIZES… THE HAND OF JESUS TOWARDS YOU."

"THANKFULNESS MULTIPLIES… HIS IDEAS TO BLESS YOU."

"HOW FAR YOU ARE FROM YOUR LAST MISTAKE…DECIDES HOW CLOSE YOU ARE TO JESUS…MENTALLY."

"HUMILITY ATTRACTS….DIVINE ATTENTION."

"YOUR REACTION TO A MAN OF GOD…IS BEING SECRETLY STUDIED BY GOD."
JESUS IS THE SWEETEST PERSON.
THE SWEETEST SPIRIT. HE IS NOT FLESHLY NOR IS HE INCONSISTENT WITH HIS PERSONALITY. HE IS LOVE. HE LOOKS BEYOND WHAT YOU DID AND GIVES YOU

MERCY AND GRACE. HE WILL WORK WITH YOU.

" JESUS DID NOT COME FOR YOU TO DIE IN SIN, BUT FOR SIN TO DIE IN YOU."

HE IS ALWAYS SPEAKING.

HIS VOICE IS A REPEATED THOUGHT THAT WILL NOT GO AWAY."

HE IS KIND, HE WILL HELP YOU AND HE TURNS NO ONE AWAY. JESUS LOVES CONVERSATION. HE LOVES SOMEONE WHO WILL GIVE HIM THEIR TIME. HE LONGS FOR A LOYAL FRIEND.

"FRIENDSHIP AND WORSHIP BIRTHS PLEASURE IN GOD."

HIS SMILES ARE CONNECTED TO YOUR
DESIRE FOR HIM.

EVERY MOMENT HE SEARCHES THE EARTH
FOR SOMEONE HUNGRY AND THIRSTY FOR
HIM. THAT WILL PURSUE HIM.

BE THAT PERSON ENGAGING THE
PRESENCE OF GOD.

THE PRESENCE OF JESUS IS THE REWARD
FOR WAITING IN PRAYER AND BEING STILL
IN WORSHIP.
"YOU ARE NOT IN PRAYER UNTIL YOU ARE
FULLY FOCUSED."
"CONCENTRATION IS GOD'S MAGNET."
"CONCENTRATION MANIFESTS GOD."
"CONCENTRATION INVITES GOD TO BE
COMFORTABLE AROUND YOU.

YOU DRAW NIGH TO GOD AND GOD DRAWS NIGH TO YOU... WHEN YOU CONCENTRATE.

DIVINE CONCENTRATION IS WHEN YOU CANCEL WHATEVER WILL SEPARATE YOU FROM JESUS.

ROMANS 8:38-39 "NEITHER DEATH, NOR LIFE, NOR ANGELS, NOR PRINCIPALITIES, NOR POWERS, NOR THINGS PRESENT, NOR THINGS TO COME, NOR HEIGHT, NOR DEPTH, NOR ANY OTHER CREATURE SHALL BE ABLE TO SEPARATE US FROM THE LOVE OF GOD, WHICH IS IN CHRIST JESUS OUR LORD."
DISTANCE FROM JESUS IS THE WILL OF SATAN.

JESUS CANNOT MANIFEST HIS WILL IN YOUR LIFE UNTIL HE SEES YOU DRAWING CLOSER

TO HIM.

THE PRESENCE OF JESUS MANIFESTS YOUR WORSHIP AND WORSHIP MANIFESTS THE PRESENCE OF JESUS.

"WORSHIP REQUIRES YOU BUT HAS NOTHING TO DO WITH YOU."

WORSHIP IS FOR JESUS. A COMPLETE FOCUS ON JESUS. WAITING ON JESUS.

THEREFORE, TRUE WORSHIP IS RARE AND LACKING. SELFISHNESS CANNOT WORSHIP. FLESH CANNOT WORSHIP. PRIDE CANNOT WORSHIP. YOU MUST DIE TO WHAT YOU FEEL, WANT, OR THINK, TO WORSHIP.

"WORSHIP IS A FRUIT OF FRIENDSHIP."

"FRIENDSHIP IS A FRUIT OF OBEDIENCE."

YOU CANNOT BE FRIENDS WITH JESUS UNTIL YOU START DOING WHAT HE SAYS.

JOHN 15:14 "YOU ARE MY FRIENDS, IF YOU DO WHAT I COMMAND."

THE PLACE OF YOUR OBEDIENCE, DECIDES THE PLACE OF YOUR FRIENDSHIP AND THE PLACE OF YOUR FRIENDSHIP, DECIDES THE PLACE OF YOUR ANOINTING.

"FRIENDSHIP WITH JESUS…ANOINTS YOU." MANY WILL NEVER WORSHIP BECAUSE THEY HAVE THE SPIRIT OF MARTHA INSTEAD OF MARY. YOU CAN ALWAYS "BE DOING," BUT NEVER DOING WHAT JESUS WANTS DONE.

WORSHIP CONSULTS GOD, WORRY INSULTS

GOD.

WORRY IS THE WRONG FOCUS. IT KILLS WORSHIP AND IT DESTROYS YOUR ATMOSPHERE WITH GOD.

"WORSHIP PURGES YOUR FOCUS."

DEPRESSION IS SELF-WORSHIP.

THE GREATEST BONDAGE IS SERVING YOURSELF AND YOUR FLESH.

WHEN JESUS IS CALLING YOU INTO SOMETHING NEW AND FRESH YOUR SILENCE INVITES GOD. GOD HAS A FASCINATION WITH A LISTENER. THOSE WHO LISTEN FOR GOD ALWAYS HAVE AN ADVANTAGE. PRAYER WITHOUT CEASING WAS NOT YOU CONSTANTLY SPEAKING, BUT

YOU CONSTANTLY LISTENING.

"GOD WILL USE SOMEONE WHO LISTENS AND IS WILLING . . . BEFORE HE USES SOMEONE WHO IS QUALIFIED."

BEING WILLING AND LISTENING QUALIFIES YOU. YOU CAN DO THINGS WITH GOD. INCLINING YOUR EAR IS THE KEY TO GETTING MANIFESTATION AND PRAYERS ANSWERED.

DECLINING YOUR EAR IS SECRET REBELLION.

SNEAKY DISOBEDIENCE WILL ENCOURAGE YOU TO RESIST GOD. RECLINING YOUR EAR IS LAZINESS. LAZINESS IS WHEN YOU KNOW WHAT WORKS, BUT DO NOT DO IT.

PRAYER WORKS ONLY FOR THE PERSON
PRAYING.

GIVING WORKS ONLY FOR THE PERSON
GIVING.

FAITH WORKS ONLY FOR THE PERSON IN
FAITH.

OBEDIENCE WORKS ONLY FOR THE PERSON
OBEYING.

BE PATIENT AND HIS PRESENCE WILL
MANIFEST WHILE YOU ARE IN PRAYER AND
WORSHIP.

DO NOT LOOK AT TIME OR HOW LONG YOU
ARE SEEKING JESUS, IT WILL TAKE YOU OUT
OF THE SPIRIT AND INTO THE FLESH.

WELCOME JESUS INTO YOUR DECISIONS;
ASK HIM FOR WISDOM AND
UNDERSTANDING. MAKE YOURSELF
AVAILABLE AND THE POWER OF GOD WILL
LIFT YOU FOREVER. GET TO KNOW THE
LORD DEEPER. LEAVE WHAT DISPLEASES

HIM AND LET JESUS TAKE YOU OVER. THIS IS YOUR TIME. FORGET ABOUT EVERYTHING. JESUS IS CALLING YOU. HIS VOICE IS SOFTLY INVITING YOU AND HIS ARMS ARE OUTSTRETCHED FOR YOU. HIS HEART IS IN LOVE WITH YOU. SURRENDER, THAT'S IT! JESUS MAKES ALL THINGS NEW. THIS IS A NEW SEASON AND LIFE FOR YOU. RECEIVE THE FULLNESS OF JESUS!

THE SECRET TO LIBERTY...IS BEING BOUND TO JESUS.
THE SECRET TO FREEDOM...IS BEING YOKED TO JESUS.

DON'T SETTLE FOR THE LEVEL YOU ARE ON. AIM FOR MORE. TARGET THE GLORY.

JESUS IS A WALKING GOD OF POWER.
JESUS IS A WALKING GOD OF GLORY.

JESUS IS A WALKING GOD OF FIRE.

JESUS WILL VISIT YOU.

VISIBLE ENCOUNTERS WITH JESUS IS YOUR INHERITANCE.

VISIBLE ENCOUNTERS WITH ANGELS IS YOUR INHERITANCE.

TRAVELING TO HEAVEN WHILE YOU ARE STILL ALIVE IN THIS BODY IS YOUR INHERITANCE.

TAKE ADVANTAGE OF THE ACCESS JESUS HAS GIVEN YOU TO HIS SUPERNATURAL WORLD.

MOVE IN IT BOLDLY AND BECOME A CHANNEL FOR HIS DIVINE POWER TO FLOW THROUGH

JHM

IX CHAPTER: PROTECTING THE PROPHETIC WHY MEN AND WOMEN OF GOD FAIL

"WHAT YOU VIEW BECOMES YOU."

WHAT YOU SEE, DECIDES WHAT YOU'LL BE."

"YOU MUST BE SERIOUS AND NOT CURIOUS."

THOSE THAT ARE CURIOUS ARE NOT SERIOUS.

"THOSE THAT DO NOT PRAY WITH THE LORD, PLAY WITH THE LORD."

YOU MUST DEVELOP FAITHFULNESS TO GOD.

"FELLOWSHIP DESTROYS THE DESIRE TO SIN AND SIN DESTROYS THE DESIRE TO FELLOWSHIP."

PROLONG YOUR FOCUS ON JESUS. EXTEND YOUR CONCENTRATION.

ATTENTIVENESS IS A SKILL.

BEING STILL BEFORE JESUS IS A GRACE.

DEMON'S DESIRE YOU…AND WHEN YOU ARE DISTRACTED THEY HAVE A MINISTRY OF STAGNATION THEY RELEASE UPON YOU.

YOU MUST GUARD YOUR EYES AND THE MEDITATION OF YOUR HEART.

THE PROPHETIC ANOINTING IS IN YOUR HEART, EVEN JESUS SAID "OUT OF THE ABUNDANCE OF THE HEART…. THE MOUTH SPEAKS." **MATTHEW 12:34** SO PROPHECY BEGINS IN THE HEART, BEFORE IT COMES OUT OF YOUR MOUTH. SO, YOUR HEART MUST BE IN THE RIGHT PLACE FOR PROPHETIC GRACE. THE PROPHETIC IS THE STRONGEST REALM OF GOD BECAUSE IT IS WHERE HE IS SPEAKING.
UNTIL GOD SPEAKS…YOU DON'T KNOW HOW TO LOVE HIM. HIS WORDS REVEAL WHETHER OR NOT YOU LOVE HIM.

"IN THE BEGINNING, GOD SPOKE… IT WAS THE PROPHETIC ANOINTING. GOD WAS

MOVING IN THE PROPHETIC IN GENESIS.
GOD WAS TEACHING ADAM THE PROPHETIC
IN GENESIS.

"YOU MUST LEAVE FEELINGS… TO HEAR
GOD."

PROTECT THE PROPHETIC ANOINTING IN
YOUR HEART. REMEMBER THAT OUT OF THE
ABUNDANCE OF YOUR HEART, YOUR
MOUTH SPEAKS.
"WHAT YOU SEE… IS A SEED."

"WHAT YOU SEE... GETS PLANTED IN YOUR
HEART."

IT AFFECTS YOUR HEART EITHER FOR
GOOD OR BAD.

AS A PROPHET, WHETHER YOU BE MALE OR

FEMALE, YOU MUST USE VIEWER
DISCRETION. KEEP WRONG STUFF AND
MATERIAL OUT OF YOUR SIGHT.

MANY PEOPLE THAT HAVE A STRONG
PROPHETIC GRACE ON THEIR LIFE, ARE
STRUGGLING WITH PERVERSION OR SEXUAL
SIN/BONDAGE. IT IS SATAN'S TRICK TO
AROUSE YOU WITH THE FLESH, SO THAT
JESUS CANNOT AROUSE YOU IN THE SPIRIT.

SATAN WANTS TO SUBSTITUTE YOUR
SPIRITUAL PLEASURES FOR FLESHLY
PLEASURES. ADAM IN THE BOOK OF
GENESIS FELT A STRONG ANOINTING, THE
GLORY OF GOD WAS STRONG ON HIM, BUT
SATAN AROUSED HIM WITH SOMETHING
ELSE.
EVERY SIN YOU STRUGGLE WITH IN YOUR
LIFE IS SENT TO KEEP YOU IGNORANT FROM

THE FULFILLMENT AND UNENDING SATISFACTION IN THE GLORY OF GOD'S PRESENCE.

THE LORD TOLD, "PROPHET ELIJAH TO GO AND HIDE BY THE BROOK CHERITH." *1 KING 17:3*

ELIJAH HAD TO PROTECT THE PROPHETIC ANOINTING ON HIS LIFE. NOTICE, THE LORD PUT THE PROPHET BY THE BROOK. WHEN GOD HIDES YOU, YOU CAN SUPERNATURALLY ACCESS THE BROOK FOR YOUR LIFE. THE BROOK OF POWER, THE BROOK OF GLORY, THE BROOK OF BLESSINGS, AND THE BROOK OF RESTORATION.
PATIENCE IS THE GPS TO YOUR PROVISION. "GOD WOULD HAVE YOU IN A SEASON OF HIDING BEFORE HE STARTS PROVIDING."

THE ANOINTING THAT YOU CARRY IS
GREAT.

HUMILITY MAKES IT GREATER

SERVANTHOOD DOUBLES IT

CONSISTENCY TRIPLES IT

ATTENTIVENESS EXTENDS IT

LOVE MATURES IT

WISDOM GUIDES IT

DISCERNMENT PROTECTS IT

REVELATION CORRECTS IT

YOUR MAN OF GOD PERFECTS IT

OBEDIENCE REFRESHES IT

WORSHIP INVITES IT…AND

FAITH IGNITES IT.

ALWAYS REMEMBER THIS, THERE IS A REALM
WHERE GOD IS OVERPROTECTIVE. YIELD TO
HIM IN THIS REALM.

ONE BAD MOVE CAN MURDER YOUR DIVINE DESTINY. BE NOT ANXIOUS, DO NOT BE IMPATIENT OR UNWILLING TO WAIT ON GOD. REMEMBER HE WAITED ON YOU YEARS TO SURRENDER, HEED, AND SUBMIT.

ANYONE THAT CONVINCES YOU NOT TO HEED DIVINE INSTRUCTIONS IS YOUR ENEMY. WHEN YOU ARE IN THIS PROCESS, DO NOT ALLOW TOO MANY PEOPLE TO HAVE ACCESS. GUARD THAT PROPHETIC FLOW WITH YOU AND JESUS.

PROVERBS 18:4 TALKED ABOUT WISDOM BEING A WELL FLOWING BROOK. WHEN PROPHET ELIJAH WAS HIDING BY THE BROOK, IT SHOWS YOU THAT WHEN GOD HAS A PROPHETIC ANOINTING ON YOUR LIFE HE WILL GIVE YOU WISDOM.

"WISDOM IS…A DIVINE BROOK FOR A PROPHET."

"WISDOM EMPOWERS THE PROPHETIC FLOW."

"WISDOM CREATES AN UNUSUAL FUNCTION OF THE PROPHETIC WHILE YOU ARE MINISTERING."

LUKE 21:15 "I WILL GIVE YOU A MOUTH AND WISDOM THAT EVEN YOUR ENEMIES CANNOT RESIST."

ELIJAH HAD A STRONG PROPHETIC GRACE, BUT GOD REQUIRED HIM TO HAVE STRONG PATIENCE. NO ONE CAN GROW IN THE PROPHETIC WITHOUT PATIENCE.

THEREFORE, JESUS ALLOWS YOU TO GO

THROUGH SEASONS OF WAITING. WAITING PERMITS, THE PROPHETIC IN YOUR LIFE.

THERE WILL BE TIMES WHEN THE HOLY GHOST WILL SPEAK TO YOU SPONTANEOUSLY, SO YOU MUST WAIT AND HAVE SPONTANEOUS LISTENING.

EVEN IN PROPHESYING YOU MUST WAIT ON JESUS TO GIVE YOU DETAILS. SO, PATIENCE KEEPS YOUR SPIRITUAL EARS WIDE OPEN. YOU MUST PRACTICE PATIENCE, FOR IT IS AN ANOINTING, THAT WELCOMES THE PROPHETIC ANOINTING.
"PATIENCE IS THE PREGNANCY OF POWER."
ISAIAH 40:31 SAYS "YOU MUST WAIT UPON THE LORD, BEFORE HE CAN RENEW YOUR STRENGTH."

RENEWING YOUR STRENGTH, MEANS

RENEWING YOUR ANOINTING.

YOU CANNOT WALK IN PATIENCE UNTIL
YOU TOTALLY SURRENDER. JOSEPH IN
GENESIS HAD EVERY STRONG PROPHETIC
MANTLE UPON HIS LIFE, BUT STILL HAD TO
ENDURE AND WAIT WITH PATIENCE FOR
GOD'S WORD TO HAPPEN IN HIS LIFE.

"PATIENCE MAKES YOUR ABILITY TO
PROPHESY SO MUCH STRONGER."

PATIENCE KILLS YOUR WILL AND IT ALSO
EXPIRES YOUR WRONG DESIRES.
THE FLESH LOSES ITS FUNCTIONALITY
THROUGH PATIENCE, NO DEMON CAN EVER
MAKE YOU SIN IF YOU DEVELOP PATIENCE.

THE DISCIPLES IN THE BOOK OF ACTS
WAITED PATIENTLY AND THEN THE HOLY

GHOST FELL WITH GREAT POWER UPON THEM. PATIENCE IS THE CAUSE FOR PROMOTION.

"IF YOU'RE IN A SEASON WHERE GOD IS HAVING YOU WAIT, IT IS BECAUSE YOUR HARVEST IS GREAT."

PATIENCE WILL CANCEL DAMAGING DECISIONS THAT YOU WILL REGRET AFTER A WHILE.

PATIENCE ALLOWS PROPHETIC GRACE TO COME UPON YOU.
ESTHER, WENT THROUGH TREATMENTS AND ASSIGNMENTS SIX MONTHS AT A TIME BECAUSE GOD WAS PREPARING HER FOR THE PROPHETIC MANTLE THROUGH PATIENCE.

AFTER SHE WENT THROUGH HER PROCESS OF PATIENCE, SHE MOVED IN A STRONG PROPHETIC ANOINTING.

THEN SHE WENT ON A THREE DAY FAST AND THE PROPHETIC ANOINTING INTENSIFIED, AND SHE WENT BEFORE THE KING WITH A PETITION TO DELIVER THE CHILDREN OF ISRAEL AND WAS SUCCESSFUL.

PATIENCE BROUGHT ESTHER INTO HER OFFICE AS QUEEN AND PROPHETESS. YOU NEED PATIENCE TO WEAR THE PROPHETIC MANTLE.
JESUS WAITED PATIENTLY THIRTY YEARS TO START HIS MINISTRY, AND THEN THE PROPHETIC EXPLODED ON HIS LIFE.

THE PROPHETIC MANTLE WAS SO HEAVY ON JESUS TO THE DEGREE, MOSES AND ELIJAH

APPEARED BEFORE HIM ON THAT
MOUNTAIN WHERE HE WAS TRANSFIGURED.

THE SCRIPTURE SAID IN **MATTHEW 17:2**
THAT WHILE JESUS PRAYED HIS FACE WAS
CHANGED AND SHINED GLORIOUSLY.

WHY DID THIS HAPPEN?

YOUR FACE REPRESENTS YOUR IDENTITY.

NOTICE LIGHT WAS ON JESUS' FACE. THE
SCRIPTURE SAYS IN **PSALMS 119:105** "THAT
THE WORD IS A LIGHT UNTO OUR PATH."
SO, WHEN YOU PRAY YOU ALLOW THE
WORD AND THE PROPHETIC ANOINTING TO
COME UPON YOUR IDENTITY. PRAYER
POSITIONS YOU TO IDENTIFY WITH THE
PROPHETIC SIDE OF GOD. THESE ARE THE
DEEP THINGS OF THE HOLY SPIRIT.

WHY DO PREACHERS OR PROPHETS FALL INTO SIN? NO MATTER HOW HIGH THE ANOINTING IS ON YOUR LIFE, YOU WILL SIN IF YOU DO NOT ENGAGE HIS PRESENCE. WHENEVER YOU ARE DISTRACTED YOU BECOME DETACHED FROM HIS DIVINE PRESENCE AND IN THIS STATE, WEAKNESS AND THE FLESH IS AT AN ALL-TIME HIGH. IF YOU GET TOO BUSY DOING ANYTHING WITHOUT CONVERSING WITH JESUS, IT WILL CREATE SIN IN YOUR DECISIONS. ONE DANGEROUS THING IS BECOMING CASUAL. MANY PREACHERS AND PROPHETS FALL BECAUSE THEY BECOME TOO CASUAL WITH THE PEOPLE THEY MINISTER. YOU MUST KEEP YOUR ASSIGNMENT AT A PROPER DISTANCE. WHEN I SAY ASSIGNMENT, I MEAN PEOPLE YOU ARE ASSIGNED TO IMPART TO AS FAR AS MINISTRY. KEEP

PEOPLE AT A DISTANCE. CASUAL CONVERSATION EMPOWERS PEOPLE TO DISRESPECT YOUR ANOINTING.

IT REMOVES THE DIGNITY OF THE GRACE YOU HAVE BEEN GIVEN. ANYTIME YOU INTERACT WITH THE OPPOSITE SEX INCREASINGLY, AND YOU ARE NOT MARRIED TO THEM YOU HAVE GIVEN PLACE TO THE DEVIL. DEMONS WILL USE THIS TO GET YOU TO LUST AND SIN WITH THAT PERSON. BEING CASUAL WILL BRING YOU INTO CAPTIVITY EVERY TIME. ANOTHER REASON WHY A PREACHER OR A PROPHET CAN START FAILING GOD IS NO CONTINUAL CONVERSATION WITH HIM. THE ABILITY TO BE STILL. THE FIRST FOUR WORDS OF FELLOWSHIP IS FELL.

MANY WOMEN AND MEN HAVE TRIED TO STAND, BUT HAVE FELL BECAUSE THEIR WAS

NOT ANY FELLOWSHIP. YOU MUST KEEP THE FLOW BETWEEN YOU AND GOD FRESH AND STRONG. THE MOMENT THAT DIES, SO DO YOU. PRACTICE BEING DILIGENT IN CLINGING TO JESUS THROUGH WAITING IN HIS PRESENCE, LISTENING FOR HIS VOICE.

ADAM TOOK HIS EYES OFF GOD AND DEVELOPED FOCUS ON SOMETHING THAT WAS WRONG. WHATEVER WEAKENS YOU OR PROMOTES WEAKNESS IS FROM THE VOICE OF SATAN. THINGS THAT WEAKEN YOU MUST BE REMOVED, CANCELLED, AGGRESSIVELY CONFRONTED BY YOU BOLDLY CLOSING WRONG PEOPLE OUT OF YOUR LIFE. MOST DISTRACTIONS COME FROM PEOPLE. MOST STRUGGLES ARE MANIFESTED THROUGH A WRONG PERSON. BE WISE, BE DISCERNING AND PURGE YOUR LIFE OF EVERYTHING PULLING YOU AWAY

FROM GOD. REPENT, THEN SEEK JESUS, PURSUE HIM IN PRAYER, ASK HIM QUESTIONS AND WAIT FOR HIS RESPONSE. PREACHERS AND PROPHET'S FALL BECAUSE OF PRIDE. WHEN IT BECOMES ALL ABOUT YOU, YOU HAVE STEPPED INTO THE SAME SPIRIT OF SATAN. SELF-SUFFICIENCY AND BEING INDEPENDENT WILL PRODUCE THE DEMONIC IN YOU. **1 CORINTHIANS 10:12** "LET HIM WHO THINKS HE STANDS, TAKE HEED, UNLESS HE FALLS."

STAYING HUMBLE EMPOWERS YOU SO YOU WILL NOT STUMBLE.
"PRIDE DOES NOT LET YOU ABIDE."
PRIDE IS A REMOVAL OF DIVINE FAVOR.

YOU CANNOT CONTINUE IN THE SPIRIT, THE ANOINTING, OR THE WILL OF GOD WHEN YOU COME INTO PRIDE.

YOU WILL FALL IF YOU LOOK TO YOURSELF, NOT JESUS.

TO OVERCOME TEMPTATION, YOUR DESIRE TO PLEASE GOD, MUST OUTWEIGH YOUR DESIRE TO PLEASE SELF.

MOSES SUFFERED WITH THE CHILDREN OF ISRAEL, INSTEAD OF ENJOYING THE PLEASURES OF SIN IN PHARAOH'S HOUSE.

"HE WANTED GOD OVER HIS FLESH. YOU MUST WANT GOD OVER YOUR FLESH, INSTEAD OF LETTING YOUR FLESH BE YOUR GOD.
"PREACHERS AND PROPHETS MISS GOD BECAUSE OF WRONG MOTIVES."

IF ANYTHING IS DRIVING YOU OTHER THAN

THE HOLY SPIRIT, YOU WILL CRASH.

EVERY COLLISION IS BECAUSE OF YOUR DIVISION WITH CHRIST. WHEN YOU ARE DIVIDED FROM HIM WRONG MOTIVES WILL EXPOSE YOU EVENTUALLY.

ANANIAS AND SAPPHIRA WERE WITH THE CHURCH WHEN THEY MOVED IN THE ANOINTING, BUT THEY LIED TO THE MAN OF GOD AND DROPPED DEAD. THEIR MOTIVES WERE WRONG, AND THEIR HEARTS WERE NOT RIGHT.
"WRONG MOTIVES TOWARDS GOD NEVER PROSPER."
YOU SHOULD WANT JESUS FOR JESUS. SERVE HIM WHEN YOU DO NOT HAVE ANYTHING OR ANYONE AND HE WILL GIVE YOU EVERYTHING YOU DESIRE.

IF YOU ARE IN MINISTRY FOR JUST FAME, OR JUST MONEY YOU WILL TRAP YOURSELF INTO DEFEAT AND DECEPTION. KEEP YOUR HEART PURE AND RUN AFTER JESUS WITH ALL YOUR LIFE, TIME, AND STRENGTH.

GIVE YOUR ENTIRE SELF TO HIM AND STAY AWAY FROM WRONG MOTIVES. FINALLY, PREACHERS AND PROPHETS PRAY HARD MOST TIMES BEFORE A SERVICE, BUT GET OFF THEIR GUARD AFTER A SERVICE. YOU MUST PRAY MORE AFTER A SERVICE THEN BEFORE A SERVICE, BECAUSE DEMONS SEEK REVENGE. THEY SEARCH FOR HOW THEY CAN RETALIATE AGAINST YOU FOR WINNING SOULS, PREACHING THE GOSPEL, AND DEMONSTRATING THE POWER OF GOD ON THE EARTH. AFTER GOD USES YOU A DEMON SPIRIT IS SOMEWHERE SEEKING TO

SEE IF THEY CAN USE YOU AFTERWARDS.
YOU MUST PRAY MORE AFTER GOD USES
YOU BECAUSE THE DEVIL KNOWS THAT IF
YOU CONTINUE AT THE PACE YOU ARE
GOING WITH JESUS AND THE ANOINTING
YOU WILL CRUSH HIS KINGDOM AND THAT
IS WHAT HE DREADS THE MOST. DO NOT
SEEK GOD JUST BEFORE A SERVICE, BE SURE
TO SEEK HIS FACE CONTINUALLY. 1
CHRONICLES 16:11

THE MOMENT YOU ARE LAZY WITH GOD IS
THE MOMENT YOU STRUGGLE AGAIN WITH
THE SIN NATURE.

"THE SIN NATURE DOES NOT DESTROY THE
ANOINTING IN YOU…
THE ANOINTING IN YOU DESTROYS
THE SIN NATURE."

Prophetic Mysteries

X CHAPTER: NETWORKING ANGELS

THE ANGELS OF GOD HAVE A NETWORK IN THE SPIRIT WHERE THEY CONNECT WITH ONE ANOTHER. THE ANGELS PARTNER TO BRING YOUR INHERITANCE TO YOU. YOUR

PERSONAL ANGEL KNOWS HOW TO
BRING OTHER ANGELS INTO YOUR
LIFE, THAT HAVE GREATER
AUTHORITY AND ACCESS TO THINGS
YOU DESIRE ON EARTH.
YOU PERSONAL ANGEL IS ALSO
KNOWLEDGEABLE OF WHAT ANGEL IS
NEEDED TO BIRTH YOUR DIVINE
ASSIGNMENT IN THE EARTH.

YOUR PERSONAL ANGEL IS WITH YOU
FROM BIRTH.
YOUR PERSONAL ANGEL HAS A NAME.
IF YOU PRAY IN THE HOLY SPIRIT OVER
YOUR ANGELS NAME, IT WILL BE
REVEALED TO YOU. YOUR PERSONAL
ANGEL HAS WISDOM OF WHAT YOU
SHOULDN'T PARTAKE OF AND WHAT
YOU SHOULD PARTAKE OF.

WHEN GOD CREATED ADAM, HE HAD PERSONAL ANGELS.

BEING THAT ADAM WAS A GOD ON THE EARTH, HIS PERSONAL ANGELS WERE CHERUBIMS.

THIS IS WHY WHEN GOD DROVE HIM OUT THE GARDEN, HE ALSO PUT CHERUBIMS TO GUARD THE GARDEN. THOSE CHERUBIMS WOULD HAVE BEEN GUARDING ADAM AND HIS WIFE.

ADAM WAS MOVING WITH THESE ANGELS BEFORE HE SINNED AGAINST GOD.

ADAM HAD POWERFUL GLORY ANGELS AROUND HIM AND HE WAS EMPOWERED BY THEM TO BE GOD TO

THE EARTH REALM.

YOUR PERSONAL ANGEL IS ALWAYS PRESENT TO HELP YOU AVOID WRONG DECISIONS , WRONG PATHS, AND WRONG PEOPLE.

YOUR PERSONAL ANGEL ENCOURAGES YOU TO OBEY THE HOLY SPIRIT.

YOUR PERSONAL ANGELS KNOW THE HARVESTS AND BLESSINGS JESUS DESIRES TO BRING TO YOU.

JESUS REVEALED SECRETS ABOUT DEMONS…HE SAID THAT WHEN THEY LEAVE YOUR BODY, THEY GO AND FIND 7 MORE WICKED SPIRITS.

NOW YOU MUST REMEMEBER A DEMON IS

AN ANGEL THAT SINNED AGAINST GOD.
NOTICE, THEY NETWORK AND FIND 7 MORE
WICKED SPIRITS.

MEANING THE DEMON THAT LEFT YOU,
WHICH IS REALLY A FALLEN ANGEL, KNOWS
HOW TO FIND 7 MORE FALLEN ANGELS
THAT ARE MORE AGGRESSIVE IN EVIL, AND
MORE CRAFTY IN DARKNESS, TO CONNECT
WITH HIM, IN ORDER TO RETURN TO YOU
WITH THINGS THAT WILL CORRUPT YOU
AND MAKE YOU MORE EVIL.

THESE FALLEN ANGELS REMEMBER THEIR
FORMER FUNCTION.

THE ABILITY TO NETWORK AND GATHER
OTHER ANGELS.

IF SATAN'S ANGELS KNOW HOW TO

NETWORK WITH ANGELS GREATER THAN THEM, IT MEANS THEY GOT THE IDEA FROM GOD.

ANGELS OF GOD KNOW HOW TO NETWORK WITH GREATER ANGELS, THAT HAVE DIVINE POWER FROM GOD TO RELEASE GREATER MONEY, GREATER MIRACLES, GREATER MANTLES, AND ALL TYPES OF HEAVENLY BLESSINGS.

WHEN YOU ARE DOING THE THINGS THE HOLY SPIRIT WANTS FROM YOU, YOUR PERSONAL ANGEL HAS THE PERMISSION TO GO AND CONTACT OTHER ANGELS IN THE HEAVENLY HOST TO JOIN YOUR LIFE.

YOUR PERSONAL ANGEL HAS THE PHONEBOOK TO EVERY ANGEL YOU NEED TO MOVE WITH IN THIS LIFE.

YOUR PERSONAL ANGEL KNOWS HOW TO
LINK YOU TO ANGELS OF PROSPERITY.

YOUR PERSONAL ANGEL KNOWS HOW TO
LINK YOU TO HEALING ANGELS.

YOUR PERSONAL ANGEL KNOWS HOW TO
CONNECT YOU TO DELIVERANCE ANGELS.

THEY HAVE THE CONTACT TO EVERY
MAJOR ANGEL THAT CAN RELEASE A
PRAYER YOU PRAYED OR GRANT A
PETITION YOU HAVE ASKED FOR.

WHEN YOU ARE STRONG IN YOUR FAITH,
YOUR PERSONAL ANGEL BECOMES AN
ENTREPRENEUR OF EVENTS THAT BIRTH
MIRACLES AND FAVORABLE OUTCOMES FOR
YOU. YOUR PERSONAL ANGEL HAS

DOMINION THAT IS ACTIVATED WHEN YOU STAND STRONG IN THE LORD AND IN THE POWER OF HIS MIGHT.

WHEN YOU ARE FOCUSED ON JESUS AND THE MAN OF GOD HE HAS PLACED IN DIVINE AUTHORITY OVER YOUR LIFE, YOUR PERSONAL ANGEL IS EMPOWERED TO GET THINGS TO YOU.

YOUR PERSONAL ANGEL CAN MOVE THE MOST WHEN YOU ARE IN HONOR.

HONOR MEANS TO CELEBRATE THE PERSON GOD IS USING TO UNLOCK YOUR ANOINTING AND GIFTS.

SOWING YOUR TIME, YOUR FOCUS, YOUR LOYALTY, YOUR MONEY, AND YOUR LIFE INTO THEM. YOUR PERSONAL ANGEL WILL

EVEN NETWORK WITH THE POWERFUL ANGELS OF A MAN OF GOD, AND THOSE ANGELS WITH THAT MAN OF GOD, WILL MOVE WITH YOU.

YOU WILL HAVE THE SAME RESULTS, FRUITS, HARVESTS, BLESSINGS, ENCOUNTERS, REVELATIONS, AND REALM THAT THE MAN OF GOD HAS.

WHEN JESUS WAS ASCENDING TO HEAVEN AFTER THE RESURRECTION, THERE WERE TWO ANGELS THAT LOOKED LIKE MEN, AND THEY HAD ON WHITE LINEN.

THEY WERE STANDING BY JESUS AND TOLD THE DISCIPLES IN ACTS THAT JESUS WOULD RETURN THE SAME WAY HE LEFT.

THEN THE WORD OF GOD SAID SOMETHING

THAT WAS HIDDEN, THAT MANY DID NOT
CATCH.

THE ANGELS DID NOT ASCEND TO HEAVEN
WITH JESUS.

ACTS 1:12 SAID…" **THEY RETURNED UNTO
JERUSALEM**.

ACTS 1:13 SAID…"**AND WHEN THEY WERE
COME IN, THEY WENT UP INTO AN UPPER
ROOM, WHERE PETER AND ALL THE
DISCIPLES WERE.**

THE POWERFUL THING WAS THAT THESE
TWO SUPERNATURAL MEN/ANGELS
FOLLOWED PETER AND ALL THE DISCIPLES
BACK TO THE UPPER ROOM.

WOW!!!!!

WHO ARE THESE TWO MEN..?

THEY ARE MOVING WITH GLORY AND FIRE.

THE REASON WHY THE GLORY AND FIRE OF
THE HOLY SPIRIT FELL SO STRONG IS
BECAUSE JESUS LEFT HIS ANGELS WITH THE
DISCIPLES.

THE ANGELS OF JESUS BEGAN TO NETWORK
WITH THE ANGELS THAT PETER AND THE
DISCIPLES HAD…AND BECAUSE PETER AND
THE OTHER DISCIPLES WERE STEADFAST IN
THEIR FOCUS ON JESUS, THEY RECEIVED
GREATER ANGELS UPON THEIR LIFE.
THEY RECEIVED GRADUATION IN THE
GLORY.

BECAUSE THEY SERVED JESUS…THEY

RECEIVED ANGELIC IMPARTATION AND BEGAN TO NETWORK WITH HIGHER RANKING ANGELS THAT HAD HIGHER AUTHORITY AND DOMINION.

IMAGINE THIS…PETER HAD TO BE OBEDIENT SO THAT HIS PERSONAL ANGELS COULD NETWORK WITH THE GLORY ANGELS JESUS WAS CARRYING.

ALSO THESE TWO MEN WERE PROPHETS IN THE GLORY THAT WERE ANGELS.

BECAUSE THE WORD OF GOD DECLARED THAT THEY WERE TWO MEN, AND THEY PROPHESIED ABOUT HOW JESUS WAS GOING TO RETURN TO EARTH, AND THAT HE WOULD DO IT THE SAME WAY HE LEFT.

THEY WERE SEERS. THEY UNDERSTAND THE

END TIMES AS WELL.

THEY KNEW AND SAW THE RETURN OF
JESUS IN THE SPIRIT REALM
PROPHETICALLY.

THESE TWO MEN WERE ELIJAH AND MOSES.
THESE WERE THE TWO MEN IN WHITE
LINEN.

THE PROPHETIC WAS SO STRONG ON PETER
BECAUSE HE HAD TWO MEN THAT WERE
MASTERS IN THE PROPHETIC FLOWING
WITH HIM. HE HAD ELIJAH ON ONE SIDE
AND MOSES ON THE OTHER SIDE.
THE POWER OF THE HOLY SPIRIT WAS SO
POWERFUL IN THE BOOK OF ACTS BECAUSE
OF THEIR PRESENCE.

ELIJAH CALLED DOWN FIRE FROM HEAVEN

IN THE OLD TESTAMENT…BUT IN THE
BOOK OF ACTS THE FIRE OF THE HOLY
SPIRIT FELL AGAIN.

THE SPIRIT OF ELIJAH WAS MOVING IN THE
DAYS OF THE OUTPOURING IN ACTS.

THESE TWO MEN WERE TWO PROPHETS
ELIJAH AND MOSES.

HERE IS A MYSTERY UNCOVERED.

JESUS' ANGELS WERE ELIJAH AND MOSES.

THIS IS WHY THEY APPEARED ON THE
MOUNTAIN OF TRANSFIGURATION.

NOTICE, **ACTS 1:10** SAID…THE TWO MEN
STOOD IN WHITE APPAREL.

WHEN JESUS WAS ON THE MOUNTAIN OF TRANSFIGURATION, TWO MEN APPEARED NEXT TO HIM…MOSES AND ELIJAH.

MARK 9:4 THERE APPEARED UNTO THEM ELIJAH AND MOSES, AND THEY WERE TALKING WITH JESUS.

SOMETHING ELSE HAPPENED, THAT WAS VERY PROFOUND.

JESUS WAS PRAYING AND **MARK 9:3** SAYS…HIS APPAREL BECAME WHITE AS SNOW.

ELIJAH AND MOSES WERE ON THE MOUNTAIN WHEN HIS GARMENTS WERE WHITE AS SNOW, AND IN THE BOOK OF ACTS THEY ARE SEEN WITH GARMENTS WHITE AS SNOW AS JESUS IS ASCENDING INTO

HEAVEN.

ELIJAH AND MOSES ALSO SHALL RETURN IN REVELATION **CHAPTER 11.**

REVELATION **CHAPTER 11:4** SAYS…"**I WILL GIVE POWER UNTO MY TWO WITNESSES.**"

NOTICE THIS IS JESUS SAYING THAT HE WILL GIVE POWER TO HIS TWO WITNESSES.

THESE ARE JESUS' ANGELS THAT HE IS GIVING POWER TO.

REVELATION 11:8 SAYS…"**THEIR DEAD BODIES SHALL LIE IN THE STREET OF THE GREAT CITY, WHICH SPIRITUALLY IS CALLED SODOM AND EGYPT, WHERE ALSO OUR LORD WAS CRUCIFIED.**"

SO ELIJAH AND MOSES ARE KILLED IN THE SAME AREA WHERE JESUS WAS CRUCIFIED.

REVELATION 11:9 SAYS…THE BODIES OF THE TWO PROPHETS WERE DEAD IN THE STREET 3 DAYS.

THEN REVELATION 11:11 SAYS…AFTER 3 DAYS THE SPIRIT OF LIFE RAISES THEM FROM THE DEAD.

REMEMBER IT WAS 3 DAYS THAT JESUS WAS DEAD THEN HE ROSE AGAIN.

REVELATION 11:12 SAYS…THEY ASCENDED INTO HEAVEN IN A CLOUD.

NOTICE MOSES AND ELIJAH TRAVELS THE SAME WAY JESUS DID BACK INTO HEAVEN…BECAUSE THESE ARE JESUS'

ANGELS.

NETWORKING ANGELS ARE SO POWERFUL.

DECIDE TO MOVE IN YOUR FAITH AT THE HIGHEST LEVEL.

DO NOT FEAR ANYTHING AND YOUR PERSONAL ANGELS WILL BE ABLE TO BRING EVEN GREATER ANGELS INTO YOUR LIFE, THAT WILL CREATE MORE FAVOR FOR YOU ON THE EARTH.

SERVING A PROPHET OF GOD, BRINGS ANGELS INTO YOUR LIFE THAT ARE GREATER IN THE GLORY AND AUTHORITY OF GOD.

WHEN YOU SOW SEEDS, YOUR ANGEL NETWORKS WITH FINANCIAL ANGELS TO

BLESS YOU.

WHEN YOU OBEY A PROPHET, YOUR PERSONAL ANGELS NETWORK WITH PROSPERITY ANGELS TO FAVOR YOU.

KEEP MOVING IN FAITH AND SPEAK THE WORD OF GOD WITH BOLDNESS, BECAUSE IT ALLOWS YOUR PERSONAL ANGEL, TO CONTACT OTHER ANGELS IN THE GLORY TO COME INTO YOUR LIFE, TO PRODUCE THE PROMISES GOD MADE TO YOU.

KEEP WALKING IN LOVE AND FORGIVENESS BECAUSE IT ALLOWS YOUR PERSONAL ANGEL TO WORK ON YOUR BEHALF.

JESUS LOVES YOU.

THIS IS A NEW BEGINNING FOR YOU.

FROM THIS MOMENT FORTH YOU ARE
UNLOCKED TO MOVE IN THE
SUPERNATURAL.

I PRAY YOUR EYES BE OPENED BY THE
POWER OF JESUS.

PRAY THIS PRAYER…

LORD JESUS, I REPENT OF MY SINS,
I FORGIVE EVERYONE IN MY LIFE,
I RECEIVE THE ANOINTING OF WISDOM
AND UNDERSTANDING, I RECEIVE MY EYES
BEING OPENED, AND I RECEIVE ANGELS
NETWORKING TOGETHER FOR YOUR
BLESSINGS TO OVERTAKE ME.
I LOOSE MY ANGEL NOW TO BRING OTHER
ANGELS IN THE GLORY INTO MY LIFE.

I RECEIVE MY INHERITANCE.

I RECEIVE MY INCREASE.

I RECEIVE EVERY ANOINTING AND EVERY ASSIGNMENT YOU HAVE FOR ME.

I RECEIVE MY PROPHET THAT IS ASSIGNED TO ME IN THE EARTH.

I RECEIVE YOUR FULLNESS.

LORD JESUS POSSESS ME.

TAKE ME OVER.

HIJACK MY BODY.

RULE MY SOUL.

I SUBMIT TO YOU COMPLETELY.

NOTES

_____

_____

_____

_____

_____

JHM

_____

_____

_____

_____

_____

_____

_____

_____

_____

_____

_____

_____

_____

NOTES

_____

_____

_____

_____

NOTES

JHM

_____

_____

_____

_____

_____

_____

_____

_____

_____

_____

NOTES

_____

_____

_____

_____

_____

_____

_____

_____

_____

_____

_____

_____

_____

_____

_____

_____

NOTES

_____

_____

_____

_____

JHM

_____

_____

_____

_____

_____

_____

_____

_____

_____

_____

_____

NOTES

_____

_____

_____

_____

_____

_____

_____

_____

_____

_____

_____

_____

_____

_____

_____

_____

NOTES

_____

_____

_____

_____

_____

JHM

_____

_____

_____

_____

_____

_____

_____

_____

_____

_____

NOTES

_____

_____

_____

_____

_____

_____

_____

_____

_____

_____

_____

_____

_____

_____

_____

_____

NOTES

_____

_____

_____

_____

JHM

_____

_____

_____

_____

_____

_____

_____

_____

_____

_____

_____

NOTES

_____

_____

_____

_____

_____

_____

_____

_____

_____

_____

_____

_____

_____

_____

_____

NOTES

_____

_____

_____

_____

JHM

_____

_____

_____

_____

_____

_____

_____

_____

_____

_____

_____

NOTES

_____

_____

_____

_____

_____

NOTES

NOTES

_____

_____

_____

_____

_____

_____

_____

_____

_____

_____

_____

_____

_____

NOTES

_____

_____

_____

_____

_____

JHM

_____

_____

_____

_____

_____

_____

_____

_____

_____

_____

_____

_____

_____

NOTES

_____

_____

_____

_____

_____

_____

_____

_____

_____

_____

_____

_____

_____

_____

_____

_____

NOTES

_____

_____

_____

_____

JHM

_____

_____

_____

_____

_____

_____

_____

_____

_____

_____

NOTES

_____

_____

_____

_____

_____
_____
_____
_____
_____
_____
_____
_____
_____
_____
_____
_____
_____

NOTES

_____
_____
_____
_____
_____

JHM

_____

_____

_____

_____

_____

_____

_____

_____

_____

_____

NOTES

_____

_____

_____

_____

_____

_____

_____

_____

_____

_____

_____

_____

_____

_____

_____

NOTES

_____

_____

_____

_____

_____

JHM

Made in the USA
Columbia, SC
09 November 2019